T0196044

LIFE Lessons from the Dying

Finding Peace and Hope in Life's Final Journey

RONALD C. DANIEL

WESTBOW
PRESS®
A DIVISION OF THOMAS NELSON
& ZONDERVAN

This book is a work of non-fiction. Unless otherwise noted, the author and the publisher make no explicit guarantees as to the accuracy of the information contained in this book and in some cases, names of people and places have been altered to protect their privacy.

WestBow Press books may be ordered through booksellers or by contacting:

WestBow Press
A Division of Thomas Nelson & Zondervan
1663 Liberty Drive
Bloomington, IN 47403
www.westbowpress.com
844-714-3454

Because of the dynamic nature of the Internet, any web addresses or links contained in this book may have changed since publication and may no longer be valid. The views expressed in this work are solely those of the author and do not necessarily reflect the views of the publisher, and the publisher hereby disclaims any responsibility for them.

Any people depicted in stock imagery provided by Getty Images are models, and such images are being used for illustrative purposes only. Certain stock imagery © Getty Images.

THE HOLY BIBLE, NEW INTERNATIONAL VERSION®, NIV® Copyright © 1973, 1978, 1984, 2011 by Biblica, Inc.® Used by permission. All rights reserved worldwide.

ISBN: 978-1-6642-0440-9 (sc)
ISBN: 978-1-6642-0439-3 (hc)
ISBN: 978-1-6642-0441-6 (e)

Library of Congress Control Number: 2020945263

Print information available on the last page.

WestBow Press rev. date: 11/28/2020

This book is dedicated to my Lord and Savior, Jesus Christ, and to my beautiful, godly wife, Laraine. Without her love, support, and encouragement, this book would not have been written. To our children, Tiffany, Meredith, and Chris, and our grandchildren, CJ, Hanna, Emma, and Preston. I love you all.

Contents

Introduction

There are many ways to experience life lessons. Most often they come simply through living. These are the ones that we can learn with each passing day as we go about our daily lives, working, playing, and enjoying interaction with others. Some life lessons come from traumatic events that occur in our lives. These can be the ones that profoundly affect us in dramatic ways and can be the most difficult to experience. Then there are other life lessons that come from spiritual experiences, such as an encounter with an angel, a spiritual awakening, or the sudden understanding of the spiritual aspects of life that you had never considered or understood in the past. They can often be the most life changing. I believe the greatest life lesson is the knowledge that God loves us, as unlovable as we are at times. Once we grasp this truth, things are never the same. As you will see, our understanding of God and His plan and purpose for each of us will greatly affect how we relate to the life lessons presented in this book.

I have titled this book *Life Lessons from the Dying* because I have spent many years with the dying. As a hospice chaplain, I have been blessed with the privilege of ministering to hundreds of terminally ill patients, their families, and their friends. During that time, I can honestly say that I have received much more from most of them than I could ever have given. I went to each of them to try to be a blessing, and I was blessed. I went to give comfort, and many times, I was the one who was comforted. I went to encourage, and I was encouraged. Most importantly, I learned that each journey to the end of life is different for every person and that each one has lessons to teach. What an amazing experience it has been.

I have told each story with as much accuracy as my memory and recall will allow. If I have made any errors in the telling, I apologize to all. However, if there are any errors of fact, I do not believe they will diminish in any way the beauty of the event or the lessons they have for us. I have also used fictitious names in each instance in order to protect the privacy of the individuals involved. Each scripture reference in this book comes from the New International Version of the Holy Bible.

It is my hope that as you read about these incredible people and their journeys, your heart and spirit will be moved in several ways. Some of their stories will bring laughter, and some will bring tears. Some will be uplifting, while others may result in deep contemplation. Hopefully, all of them will help you to see life and, yes, even death in a different light.

It is also my desire that as you read the true life and death experiences I have shared in this book, you too will learn life lessons as I did. Some may be the same I learned, but some may be entirely different. I have also left a page titled "Reflections" after each story, with the hope that you will put into your own words what each one has said to you. So let us enter this most unique classroom and see what nuggets of knowledge we can find.

CHAPTER 1

The Heart of a Servant

The trip out to my new patient's home was a pleasant one. It was an early fall afternoon with the leaves just beginning to change their colors. There was a crispness in the air. It was one of those days that make autumn so special. My patient, Russ, lived with his wife in a beautiful home sitting in the midst of large hardwoods. It was a very rustic and comfortable-looking house. I realized that the peace of their surroundings would not likely be found in their home.

After arriving, I walked up onto the porch and rang the doorbell. I was met by the patient's wife, Samantha, who welcomed me in with a smile. As she led me into the family room, I was surprised to see several men and women dressed in fire department uniforms. I was alarmed at first, thinking that there was an emergency situation happening. Then Russ explained that he was a firefighter and these were some of the team members from his station who had come by to visit with him. After a lot of hugs and words of encouragement, they all left, and I had my first opportunity to sit down and talk with the couple.

Russ looked like anything but a hospice patient. He was a large man, very healthy looking, with a ready smile. He had been diagnosed with cancer and there were no longer any treatments that could help him. Even though he knew he was on the last days of his earthly journey, he wanted to make the most of them. His plan was for him, his wife, and their families to enjoy as much of their time together as they could. Russ explained that they both came from large families and his had lived in the area for several generations. Having grown up and gone to school

1

there, he knew pretty much everyone in the county. He and Samantha were blessed to have such great support from family, friends, and their church.

When I asked Russ about his career as a firefighter, his eyes lit up and he told me he had wanted to be a firefighter for as long as he could remember. As soon as he was age eligible, he joined the department. He had been a firefighter for over twenty years. I could hear the excitement in his voice and see the passion in his eyes when he spoke of this. He had always wanted to serve and protect his community, and he was certain this was the path God had chosen for him. Sadly, he could no longer carry out the duties of a firefighter, and he was having a very difficult time adjusting to the changes this had brought about in his life.

Russ also had a passion for hunting. He just loved to be out enjoying nature, and he never killed just to be killing. It was the thrill of the hunt he enjoyed the most. If he killed a deer, most of the meat would go to friends and family. Russ not only had a servant's heart but was also a generous man.

Russ and Samantha both loved the Lord and had a rock-solid faith. They served faithfully in the church where Russ had attended for his entire life. Russ told me more than once that he was not afraid of dying. He knew he was right with God because of his faith in Jesus Christ. He was secure in his eternal destination. As is usually the case though, for all men who love their wives, Samantha's well-being was his major concern.

Samantha quietly sat beside Russ as we talked. When I turned the conversation toward Russ's illness, she began to open up and express her feelings about how difficult their struggles had become. She couldn't envision a future without her husband. He was the love of her life just as she was his. They had known each other for years and gone to school together, knowing that one day they would marry. They had no children, so it had always been just the two of them. She said that until someone had experienced a situation such as theirs, a person could never understand the stresses it puts on every area of life for the entire family.

As I visited with them over the next few weeks, it was obvious that Russ was declining. He had become much weaker, and it almost seemed as if he was shrinking as the cancer continued to feed off his body. Despite this, his spirit and his faith remained strong. In fact, I was amazed when I arrived at their home one day and he told me he had gone hunting a few days before. I couldn't imagine how he had the strength to do this, but he explained that God had given him the supernatural strength he needed to go with a friend one more time. He knew it would be his last.

Russ finally succumbed to his illness. He stepped peacefully and bravely into eternity. I was very honored when Samantha asked me to participate in his funeral. I had no idea what I was about to experience as a result.

The service had to be moved to the largest church in the area because their pastor knew that their sanctuary would not be large enough to hold all the people who would be attending. It was a cool but sunny day as people began entering the worship center that would hold nearly two thousand people. It was an amazing attendance as family, friends, and first responders came to honor a man who was loved and respected by all who knew him. As I sat on the platform and looked out over the worship center, I saw that there was not one empty seat. It was a standing room only crowd. I had to wonder what the fire marshal would have to say about this under normal circumstances.

As the service began, it became apparent that this was going to be a celebration. Many people came to the podium to share memories of Russ, some bringing laughter and others bringing tears. With it all, there was still a celebratory atmosphere—for Russ's life and his homegoing. He had touched more lives in a positive way, more than we will ever know this side of heaven.

When it came time for me to speak, I stepped up to the podium and was almost overwhelmed by what I saw. Almost half the seats in that large worship center were filled with first responders in uniform, including firefighters, police officers, and EMTs. They had all come to honor a fallen comrade. I don't remember much of what I said that day, but I do remember telling them that they were the true American heroes. It wasn't the rock stars, the professional athletes, or the movie stars that so many people seemed to idolize. Our people serving in the military and our first responders, all who risked their lives every day for our sake, were the real heroes. I told them how Russ was one of my heroes, not just because he had been a firefighter for so many years but because of his faith, his servant's heart, and the brave manner in which he faced the end of his life.

I believe that most people left the service feeling uplifted and in awe of the love and respect that was bestowed on Russ that day. I thought of how proud of her husband Samantha must have been, even in the midst of her grief and sense of loss. Russ may have been gone, but his memory and his legacy would continue on.

I didn't know it at the time, but the amazing tribute to him was not over. When I stepped into the late afternoon sunshine, I was amazed to see numerous fire trucks lined up in the parking lot, followed by emergency response units, ambulances, and police cars. It truly was an impressive sight. Then I noticed one lone fire truck pulled up to the curb just outside of the worship center doors. It was at that moment the pallbearers came out the door, and Russ's casket was lifted to the top of the fire truck. This would be his final ride on one.

It was a procession like I had never been in before. Police cars were in front and back of the procession, with lights flashing. I cannot even begin to guess how many emergency vehicles were in the line, but it was a sight that brought tears to my eyes. Each intersection had been blocked off by fire trucks, allowing safe passage for the procession that must have gone on for blocks. When we arrived at the cemetery, another fire truck was parked next to the entrance, with its ladder extended high in the sky and an American flag attached to the end and gently blowing in the breeze.

The fire truck that was carrying Russ's casket was parked as closely as possible to the gravesite. Hundreds of people were gathered around. Several more people spoke briefly, and when they had finished, there was a moment of silence. Suddenly, that silence was broken by the sound of a siren in the distance. As soon as it had become quiet, the speakers on the fire truck next to the gravesite announced that Russ had answered his final call. We all stood in stunned silence as the closing prayer was offered.

By the time the service was over, the sun was sinking low over the horizon and the temperature had dropped considerably. I returned to my car and sat with the heater running, but it would be at least a half hour before I could get out of the cemetery because of the number of cars in line. This gave me a little time to process what I had just experienced. I realized that to be a part of such a memorable service was one of the most humbling experiences of my life. I also recognized that I had been in the presence of hundreds of heroes, people like Russ who were willing to sacrifice their lives for others. I spent a moment in prayer for all of them, for Samantha, and for their families. Finally, it was time to go home and tell my wife, once again, how much I love and appreciate her.

LIFE LESSON

Who are your heroes? A person doesn't have to be a first responder or in the military to be a hero. A person doesn't have to perform some brave act to be a hero. Let me give you some examples of my heroes. First and foremost is Jesus, who has already given His life for me; my wife; caregivers; nurses; the person who keeps an eye out for the elderly neighbor next door; and the one who does a random act of kindness each day, just for the fun of it. The list could go on and on, but I think you get the idea.

Heroes are all around us, and they don't necessarily wear a uniform. In fact, you are probably a hero to someone and don't even know it. It could be your children or your grandchildren. You could be a hero to your coworker or next-door neighbor. Maybe you have been a hero to someone who was having a bad day and you offered a smile or a kind word.

You see, I believe that one of the most important qualities of a hero is to have a loving, servant's heart. Even Jesus thought so.

> Then the King will say to those on his right, "Come, you who are blessed by my Father; take your inheritance, the kingdom prepared for you since the creation of the world. For I was hungry and you gave me something to eat, I was thirsty and you gave me something to drink,

I was a stranger and you invited me in, I needed clothes and you clothed me, I was sick and you looked after me, I was in prison and you came to visit me." (Matthew 25:34–36)

Not so with you. Instead, whoever wants to become great among you must be your servant, and whoever wants to be first must be slave of all. For even the Son of Man did not come to be served, but to serve, and to give his life as a ransom for many. (Mark 10:43–45)

REFLECTIONS

CHAPTER 2

Three Beautiful Flowers

The majority of the patients we received into our inpatient unit were what our society would consider to be elderly. I prefer to call them marvelously mature since I can now be counted among them. Most would testify to having lived productive and fulfilling lives.

One morning I arrived at the inpatient unit to discover we had admitted a female patient in her twenties who had been diagnosed with terminal brain cancer. By the time she was sent to us, she was no longer responsive. Even before seeing the patient and her family, I knew this was going to be one of those cases that I would never forget. I reviewed the chart and talked with the social worker and nurse before going down the hall to do my spiritual assessment. As I walked toward the patient's room, I did what I always do. I prayed.

When I entered the room, the patient was lying so still you would have thought she had already passed, except for a very slight movement of the sheet as a result of her very shallow but regular breathing. I confirmed that the man and woman in her room were her father and mother. They sat in total silence, as if they were afraid any sound would awaken their sleeping child or be a desecration of the silence. The father was sitting on the couch at one end of the room, and the mother was sitting in a chair closest to her daughter's bed. I immediately sensed a tension in the room that extended beyond that of parents sitting at the bedside of a dying child.

During my assessment, I learned that the parents were divorced, and the divorce had been a very contentious one. However, the imminent death of one of their children had brought them together in a way neither of them could ever have imagined. The mother was an attractive woman with a very serene demeanor, especially under the circumstances. The father, on the other hand, was a huge, muscular man, somewhat intimidating in appearance. I learned as the days passed that he was a gentle giant, a big teddy bear. Of one thing there could be no mistake. They both loved their dying child with a passion. I could not even begin to imagine what they must have been feeling as they watched the life drain from their beautiful daughter. At times during my visits, they would reveal some of their thoughts and impressions, but for the most part, they appeared to be internalizing most of them, which could be cause for concern.

As I observed the parents interacting with one another over the next few days, I noticed other dynamics at work. When their daughter had first arrived at the inpatient unit, I could sense the controlled hostility between them, but as time passed, I began to see a softening of their responses to each other. At first there was very little interaction and hardly any eye contact, but this also began to change. I soon realized that I was not only ministering to parents who were hurting beyond my ability to comprehend, I was watching God at work, possibly using a heartbreaking tragedy in a way I could never have imagined. Was God using the impending death of a daughter to bring healing to a broken marriage, or was I just being a sentimental romantic? One thing I have learned over the years: never discount anything God can and will do, no matter what the circumstances.

I also learned this was a family of faith. They prayed for healing for their daughter, but they had accepted the reality that healing in this life might not come. They prayed with great courage for God's will to be done in her life, whatever it may be, recognizing that when she passed, she would instantly be healed and in the presence of the Lord Jesus Christ who loved her even more than they ever could. There were times when I would leave the patient's room, marveling at the demonstration of faith I was seeing and wondering if my faith could be that strong in the same circumstances. I was convicted at times at how easily my faith could be shaken and how weak it seemed when challenged with much smaller trials than theirs. I was in God's school now. Without them knowing it, God was using this young patient and her parents to teach valuable lessons to me and other staff members.

As the days passed and they continued their death watch over their daughter, the relationship between the two continued its metamorphosis. They became more relaxed in their interaction, even able to laugh and to share memories. I also noticed that the father kept making innuendos relating to a possible reconciliation with his wife. He would make remarks about this and then watch and listen to see how she would respond. More than once I saw her roll her eyes or shake her head, but I also noticed she often did this with a smile that had not been there before. I have to admit that I was like a person who is reading a book that has so caught his interest he can't put it down. I couldn't wait to see the ending.

One day I entered the room, and the father was sitting silently, staring in the direction of his daughter, who was peacefully lying in bed. Her mother was not present. He didn't seem to notice I had entered, but I felt I might be interrupting a very special time between him and his daughter so I began to quietly back out the room. It was then that he saw me and invited me to come in. As I did, I looked at his daughter, and I was certain I was looking at an angel. Her complexion was beautiful, not showing any signs of the destruction taking place in her body. Her hair was spread out on the pillow as if someone had staged it that way. In fact, I was almost certain I saw a luminous radiation around her. She truly looked angelic. I was stunned for a moment, and all I could do was stare.

When I was finally able to take my eyes away from her, I asked the father if he would mind telling me what he was thinking as he was watching his daughter. I wasn't sure there were words that could express his thoughts, but I hoped he would try. He sat silently for a few minutes that seemed like hours, not acknowledging my question, and I was beginning to think I had invaded an area that was off limits. Even though it was becoming uncomfortable, I waited without making a sound, holding my breath, anticipating the explosion that might come. Finally, this giant of a man looked at me with eyes filled with love for his daughter and said, "You know, chaplain, God gave me three daughters, three beautiful flowers, and if He chooses to pick one for His garden, who am I to argue?"

It was as if time had stopped. There was not a single sound. There was only him, me, and his dying daughter, and I felt as if there were no one else in the world. I was stunned to the point of speechlessness. I knew there was not a single thing I could say in response to what he had just shared. I thought that I had never heard anything so profound and so beautiful. I could feel the lump in my throat, and tears were welling up in my eyes. Because I felt this was a holy moment, I finally said in a whisper, "Thank you for sharing that with me." I quietly rose and left him to spend more time with his beautiful flower before God picked her and took her home to bloom so much more beautifully in His garden. God did his gardening the next day.

Did God use their daughter's illness and ultimate death to bring this couple back together? I wish I knew. I really am a romantic, so I have imagined in my own story that He did. In fact, I have often envisioned her looking down from heaven with a smile on her face and joy in her heart and hearing Jesus say, "Well done, good and faithful servant!" (Matthew 25:21).

LIFE LESSON

As a chaplain who has served in both a hospital and a hospice, I have ministered to the friends and loved ones of young people who have died. The questions are usually the same. Why did they die so young? Why would God take someone who had so much promise and so much life to live? What good could come from this?

Maybe God had a higher use for them in heaven. Maybe He would use their lives, as short as they seemed to be, to encourage others to examine their lives and their eternal destinations. Or maybe God was sparing them the pain we sometimes experience in this life. Since I am not God, I'm not sure I know the right questions. I'm certain I don't know the right answers.

One thing I do know. God has a plan and purpose for everything He does. We may not see it in this life, we may not appreciate it, but God's mercy and grace are at work even in these situations.

"And we know that in all things God works for the good of those who love him, who have been called according to his purpose" (Romans 8:28). Whatever God allows to happen in our lives will always work for our good and for His glory.

REFLECTIONS

CHAPTER 3

The Week of a Lifetime

I received the phone call late on a Sunday evening. As a hospice chaplain, I usually expected late-night calls to be bad news. I anticipated that this call could result in a long night with a family who had lost, or soon would lose, a loved one, and they wanted the chaplain to be present with them. I accept this, because this is who we are and what we do as chaplains. We were called by God to a unique ministry, and we see it as an honor and a privilege to be able to serve the Lord by serving others in such difficult times. I had no idea this phone call would begin a series of events that would forever change my life and the lives of others.

The call was from one of our admission nurses. He had just admitted a home patient with terminal lung cancer, and even though the patient had just been diagnosed a few days before, he was only given a few days to live. The nurse explained that the patient and his significant other wanted to get married before he died. My very first thought was *This is not going to happen.* I had received this kind of request several times before, and in each case, the patient had died before everything could be arranged. I told the nurse that the patient and his significant other would have to go to the courthouse to get a license before I could perform the ceremony. He explained that the patient was too sick to do this. He also told me that the significant other wanted to speak with the chaplain that night, if at all possible. I assured him I would call her and explain the logistical problems we faced.

Jan, the significant other, immediately answered the phone when I called the number given to me by the nurse. She explained that she and the patient, Mike, had been together for seven years and had often talked about getting married, but somehow it just never happened. Since they had been told he only had a few days to live, he had been busy taking care of financial and other personal matters from his bed. The last thing on his to-do list was to marry Jan before he died. As I listened to Jan, my spirit was moved in a way I cannot explain. I didn't know at the time if it was the plea in her voice or the work of the Holy Spirit, but I would soon receive my answer.

I explained to Jan that she and Mike would have to go to the courthouse to obtain a marriage license. Of course she told me the same thing the nurse had just related. There was no way Mike could get out of bed and do this. As we talked, I had an epiphany. I suddenly knew this marriage was supposed to happen. It was then I suggested that it might be possible to have Mike transported to the courthouse by ambulance, but I warned Jan it would be a very expensive trip. She reminded me that even if he got to the courthouse by ambulance, he would not be able to go into the clerk's office to sign the application. Showing no concern about the cost or the obstacles, she pleaded with me to do whatever I could to make this happen. I promised her I would start working on it first thing the next morning.

I had a very sleepless night after our conversation. I spent most of the night going over several different scenarios of how we could make this wedding take place. I was up and off to the office early the next morning, anxious to get things started. When I arrived, I explained the situation to our inpatient social worker. She was also excited about the opportunity and offered to call a local ambulance company we often used at hospice. We first needed to determine if an ambulance would be available and what the cost would be for transporting the patient from his home to the courthouse and back home again. I was floored when she came back and reported her conversation with the ambulance company. When she explained the circumstances to them and what we were trying to do, they offered to transport the patient free of charge! I then realized that God's hands were all over this. God was going to make it happen. Not me, but God. I was just a small cog in the big machine.

I couldn't wait to call Jan and let her know the good news, but first I had to call the clerk of court who issued the marriage licenses to see if she could come out to the ambulance once the patient arrived in order to obtain Mike's information and get his required signature. Even more importantly, I needed to know if she could expedite the processing of the application and issuing of the license. This one phone call was all it took to take away my euphoria. In all my enthusiasm, I had forgotten it was a holiday and the office was closed until the next day! I couldn't believe it. We may not have another day. Mike could go into a coma or die before then. How could this happen?

As I look back on this experience now, I know God must have been shaking His head at my reaction. A few minutes before, I was convinced God was going to make this wedding happen, and now one simple obstacle was causing me to doubt. Once again I was in God's school, and He hadn't even begun to teach me what I needed to learn. In fact, He was about to really show off!

I called Jan to give her both the good and the bad news. Since I had not met her or Mike face-to-face, I asked her if I could come visit with them for a few minutes, and she was agreeable. I prayed as I drove to their apartment. In fact, I was so focused on prayer that I don't remember the drive. I apologize to anyone whose life I may have endangered during that trip, but I was on a mission from God.

When I arrived at their apartment, Mike was in a hospital bed in the living room. Jan was present with several other family members. Mike and Jan were such likeable people that I instantly fell in love with them both. They reminded me of leftover hippies. Jan dressed the part, and Mike certainly looked the part with his long hair and bushy beard. They were free spirits, and the love they had for one another was evident.

I learned that Mike had been a police officer for most of his working life. He had once served as a hostage negotiator and later the police chief in a small town in Alaska. Interestingly enough, his daughter who was also present had come from Alaska to be with him when she learned he was dying. God does work in strange and mysterious ways, because Mike had not known about her until a short time before, when she found him on the internet.

Part of our ministry as hospice chaplains is to determine where a patient is spiritually so we can assist them in following the path they have chosen. When I asked Mike to tell me about his relationship with God, he responded that he didn't have one. When I asked why, he answered that he had done a lot of bad things in his life and didn't think God could forgive him. Additionally, he had pretty much lived his entire life without God, and he wasn't going to ask God to save him now because that would be hypocritical.

This was quite a speech for a man who could hardly breathe, even though he was receiving a high amount of oxygen. When he was finished, I began to tell him about God's unlimited and unconditional love and that it didn't matter where he had been or what he had done. God's grace is bigger than all his sin. I could see the tears welling up in his eyes as I spoke. Then I explained about forgiveness of sin and eternal life that could only be obtained through faith in Jesus Christ, the One who had shed His blood and given His life as payment for our sins.

The room was totally silent. I could see that Mike's family members were holding their collective breaths as I asked him if he would like to surrender his life to Jesus and receive forgiveness of his sins and the gift of eternal life. It was as if even the angels were silently waiting for his response. Mike's eternal destination hung in the balance, and all I could do at that point was pray.

I watched the tears begin to run down his face, and after what seemed like an eternity, Mike responded that he would. In the stillness of that moment, Mike asked Jesus to forgive him of his sins and to be his Lord and Savior. I knew at that instant that God was in that place, and the heavens were rejoicing. But that wasn't the only rejoicing going on. Mike's family members were crying and rejoicing at the same time. I wasn't aware until later that Jan and Mike's entire family had been praying desperately that he would be saved before he died. God had heard them, and He had answered.

I told them I would call the clerk of court as soon as the office opened the next morning, which would be Tuesday. As I left their apartment where the family was still celebrating, I couldn't help but think that whether or not Mike and Jan were able to be married, God had already taken care of the most important thing. Mike was on his way to heaven. *But God* (isn't that a wonderful phrase?) was just beginning to show His stuff.

The next morning, I called the clerk of court's office as soon as it opened and explained the situation. The clerk was all that we could have hoped for and more. She offered to do all that we had asked. As soon as the ambulance arrived, she would go out to it to get the information and signature she would need. She would then expedite the processing of the marriage license. She would be waiting for us to arrive and would immediately put everything into motion. Our social worker then called the ambulance company and made arrangements for them to pick up the patient and his wife-to-be. They would arrive at the courthouse within the next hour.

I left for the courthouse on a cloud, heart racing and mind working overtime, trying to think of anything I may have missed. In the midst of all this, I was praising and thanking God for what He had already done.

I arrived at the courthouse, met with the clerk, and informed her the ambulance was on its way. Then I took a seat in an open area of the building so I would be able to see the ambulance when it arrived. It was then that the reality of what I had set in motion began to hit me, and I have to admit to almost having a panic attack. If this wedding really took place without a hitch, I could look like a hero. If something went wrong, I could look like a complete fool and maybe even lose my job. I also realized I had not received authorization to move a patient. I then started trying to reach some of my superiors to let them know what I had done, but it was a little late. An old phrase came to mind: "Sometimes it is easier to ask forgiveness than it is to ask permission."

Before I had left our inpatient unit that morning to come to the courthouse, I had tried to contact the local newspaper, thinking they might want to cover the wedding since it would be such a good human-interest story. It could also generate some good publicity for the company for whom I worked, as well as the ambulance company. Unfortunately, all I could do was leave a message for the reporter. I didn't know if we would have any coverage or not, but our case manager (the patient's nurse) was coming to meet us at the courthouse and take care of her patient and hopefully take some pictures. I was just looking for a little coverage because I felt that this was the kind of feel-good story that appeals to a lot of people. *But God* (there's that phrase again) had much bigger plans, as I would soon find out.

As I sat waiting for the ambulance, my cell phone rang. It was one of the EMTs on the ambulance informing me they had arrived. I told them that I was looking out at the street in front of the courthouse and didn't see them. It seems that they had parked at the fire station around the corner. I explained that I really needed them to park on the street right in front of the courthouse because the clerk of court would have to come out of the courthouse to the ambulance. This was a very busy street, but the EMT agreed to pull in front of the courthouse and put their lights on, and hopefully the police would not bother us. Shortly after we hung up, the ambulance, with its emergency lights flashing, pulled right across the street, directly in front of the courthouse door. I notified the clerk, and things began to happen.

I went out to the ambulance and met the three EMTs who had brought the couple to the courthouse. When they opened the back of the unit, there sat the blushing bride next to the groom. Mike was lying on the gurney with his oxygen going full blast. Even at that, he was having difficulty breathing. Family members began to arrive in their cars. With the ambulance sitting in front of the courthouse with its lights flashing, we drew a crowd of people wanting to know what was going on. The case manager also arrived and climbed into the ambulance to check on her patient. Everything was well for the moment, and she began to take a few pictures. The clerk, who had come out to the ambulance as well, had begun getting all the information and signatures she would need to prepare the marriage license.

While I was standing at the back of the ambulance and speaking with the EMTs, and the family members were talking with the bride and groom, I saw a man walking down the street with a large camera on his shoulder. I thought, *Thank You, God, for sending someone from the newspaper to cover this special event.*

But God (I know you've heard this before) was about to show me that I was thinking too small. He had much larger plans. The man with the camera walked up to me and asked what was going on. I told him we were about to have a wedding, and he asked where. I told him the wedding would take place in the ambulance, and I explained the circumstances. I then asked if he was from the local newspaper, and he said he wasn't. I was somewhat disappointed until he turned his camera over so I could see that he was with the most watched local TV station in our city. This station was an affiliate of one of the three top TV networks! He had been up the street in the town square to cover the making of a movie that was being filmed there. He just happened to come upon us as he was returning to his truck.

The cameraman asked if I thought the couple would mind if he videotaped the wedding. I wasn't sure how they would feel about this, but I said I would seek their permission. I climbed into the ambulance and said, "Neither of you are fugitives from the law, are you? This man is from a TV news program and would like to tape your wedding."

They were ecstatic and quickly gave their permission. As I was telling the cameraman that it was okay to tape the wedding, the reporter himself, one of the best known in the city, walked up and asked what was going on. I again explained what we were doing and told him that we were just waiting for the clerk to return with the license so we could begin the wedding. He asked if the couple would mind him covering the wedding and having it aired on the evening news. I was totally shocked. Once again I received their permission. The crowd was growing bigger, and so was my amazement at what God was doing.

The reporter told me he had to go into the courthouse for just a minute and asked that we not start until he returned. I requested that he hurry because of the patient's condition. I wasn't sure what effect all the excitement might be having on him. Flashing through my mind was a very ugly picture of him dying just before the wedding—or even worse taking his last breath on camera in the middle of the ceremony. At this point, with so much hanging in the balance, I considered that I might be the one to fall over with a heart attack before this was over.

The clerk soon returned with the license, and the reporter was close behind. Before we began the ceremony, the reporter told me that the wedding was the buzz throughout the entire courthouse. When I turned to look at the courthouse, people were lined up at all the windows for several floors, watching what was taking place. In addition, the crowd outside had continued to grow. It had become a very festive occasion.

It was finally time to start. I climbed back into the ambulance and sat on the bench next to the bride, who was holding the groom's hand as he struggled to breathe. As the crowd watched and the camera rolled, the impossible became possible. We had a wedding! When it was over, the news reporter briefly interviewed the newlyweds, along with family members. Then the patient and his new wife were quickly and safely returned to their home. Mike went into a coma shortly after returning home. He had completed his to-do list. All that was left now was to take that final journey home to be with the One who pursued Him with a relentless love. On Thursday morning, Mike went to be with the Savior in whom he had placed his faith only three days before. I was honored to be able to officiate at his memorial service on Saturday. Saved on Monday, married on Tuesday, went to be with the Lord on Thursday, and his life celebrated on Saturday. It truly was the week of a lifetime.

You might think this is the end of the story, *but God* (I just can't say it enough) wasn't through. The story was aired on the evening news that Tuesday night and the next Wednesday morning. Another airing was done as a follow-up story announcing his death. The original video that was aired on Tuesday night made its way to YouTube and went viral, eventually making its way around the world! On the night I had received that initial phone call, I had only seen the impossible, *but God* demonstrated once again that He is the God who makes the impossible possible.

LIFE LESSON

Jesus reminds us in Mark 10:27 that "all things are possible with God." Often we look at what appear to be impossible situations in our own lives and believe they are too big for God to handle. We see hopelessness, but God sees unending hope. This is why Paul was able to write with confidence, "Be joyful in hope, patient in affliction, and faithful in prayer" (Romans 12:12). Think of what God could accomplish in our lives if we truly believed in His unlimited power and acted accordingly, in faith. Is there anything in your life right now that seems hopeless? Turn it over to the God of all hope, and see what He can do.

REFLECTIONS

CHAPTER 4

A Modern-Day Love Story

They were both in their eighties, but if I ever saw an example of growing old with dignity, they certainly met all the criteria. Even though Frank and Bernice had hoped for children in the early years of their marriage, they were never blessed with any. They accepted, in faith, that this was God's will. They had considered adopting, but somehow the time passed and it never happened. As Frank told me, they became too busy with life.

I visited with them in their home, and they were so hospitable, even in the midst of their very difficult circumstances. Bernice had been diagnosed with terminal cancer, and even though she had tried all the treatments suggested by her doctors, all had failed to stop the relentless advance of her disease. I could see her deteriorating a little more at each visit. I could also see that, as her health and her body continued to diminish, their love and affection for one another seemed to be increasing. It was a sad but most beautiful thing to watch. I was privileged to observe this indomitable power of love in action.

Eventually Bernice reached the point in her illness that Frank could no longer care for her at home, and she was admitted to the inpatient unit. She continued to exhibit a wonderful sense of humor and offered the sweetest smile and a word of encouragement to everyone who visited her. Frank was always at her side, holding her hand, speaking comforting words, telling her he loved her, and doing whatever he could to help make her more comfortable.

In her healthy days, Bernice had been a very talented painter. In addition, she enjoyed crocheting beautiful pieces she often gave away to others. Frank brought several pieces of her beautiful creations to adorn the room and for others to enjoy. Everyone who entered her room was awed by her labors of love. She was very humble when talking about them and the many hours it took to complete each work of art, but Frank would be bursting with pride as he stood by.

Bernice began to sleep more each day and eventually became unresponsive. I sat with Frank in her room on one of those quiet mornings and listened as he shared some long-ago but very precious memories. He related that he and Bernice had been introduced to each other by her cousin when they were both in their teens. Back in those days, as he described them, their dating consisted of his walking her home from church while under the watchful eye of her parents. He smiled as he shared this, and I could see the tears gathering in his eyes.

Before their relationship had the opportunity to advance much further, Frank answered the call to military service. When it was time for him to go overseas, Frank didn't ask Bernice to wait on him, because he didn't feel it would be fair to her. Secretly he hoped and prayed that she would. Months went by, and Frank and Bernice exchanged letters regularly, even though their delivery would sometimes be delayed for weeks at a time. Like others in his same situation, he always feared receiving what was often called a "Dear John letter."

When it was finally time for Frank to return home, he had not yet received the last letters Bernice had written to him, so he wasn't sure what he would find when he arrived. Had she waited for him? Was she even interested in continuing a relationship with him? With a huge smile, Frank told me of his great joy when he saw her for the first time after returning home. Not only had she waited, but they had now been married over sixty of the best years of his life.

As Bernice approached her last days, Frank continued to stay closely by her side. He read the Bible to her and told her over and over how much he loved her and what a wonderful wife she was. One morning as I entered her room, I overheard him telling her that she was more beautiful today than she had been on the day he had married her. It was such an intimate moment that I quietly backed out of the room with tears in my eyes. A few hours later, with her husband holding her hand, she went home to be with the Lord she loved so much. Tears ran down Frank's weathered and wrinkled face as he told her he would be joining her soon. I stood with my arms around his shoulders, in the silence of a holy moment. As I later reflected on this sweet couple and the example they had lived out, I knew I had seen a true modern-day love story.

LIFE LESSON

The apostle Paul, under the inspiration of the Holy Spirit, wrote,

> Love is patient, love is kind. It does not envy, it does not boast, it is not proud. It is not rude, it is not self-seeking, it is not easily angered, it keeps no record of wrongs. Love does not delight in evil but rejoices with the truth. It always protects, always trusts, always hopes, always perseveres. Love never fails. (1 Corinthians 13:4–8)

True love knows no boundaries, not even the boundaries of time. True love continues to grow and flourish through the passing of time and the challenge of great difficulties. True love such as this is a priceless treasure that never ends, even with the loss of the one who was the object of that love.

REFLECTIONS

CHAPTER 5

The Beauty That Comes with Age

When I first saw the profile of the new home patient admitted in my territory, I immediately did something I often warn others not to do. I made an assumption, and we all know the danger of making assumptions. The new patient was a 101-year-old female. My assumption was that my visits and ministry would probably be more for the caregivers than the patient. In my mind, I pictured a bedridden, unresponsive patient and a large, grieving family that included children and maybe a few great-great-grandchildren thrown in. It wasn't long before I was once again taught a valuable lesson about how wrong assumptions can be.

On my first visit, I learned that the patient lived with her great-niece and the niece's family, which included a husband, two sons, a daughter, and a dog. There may also have been a cat, but with all the activity constantly going on in the house, I may have missed it.

Rather than being bedridden and unresponsive, the patient was sitting in her favorite chair next to a sliding glass door in the family room. She was very alert and looking forward to a visit from the chaplain. Her great-niece pulled a kitchen chair right next to the patient's chair and invited me to have a seat. She explained that the patient was very hard of hearing, so even at that close range, I would have to speak loudly. Then the family also settled into the family room to listen to what the chaplain had to say. Not knowing the patient or the family very well at that time, I felt like a bug under a microscope.

When I began to speak loudly to the patient, I quickly found that even though she was 101 years old, her mind was as sharp as any I had ever encountered. She had a quick wit and a wonderful sense of humor. Over time, I learned that she could quickly put me in my place and make me feel like a child being scolded by an adult. She also had 101 years' worth of experiences to share, as well as a wealth of wisdom. As our relationship grew, I was reminded once again of how much younger people often miss by not spending time with the older generation. They are a treasure, living history, with so much knowledge and valuable lessons to share if given the opportunity.

The patient, whom I'll call Joy because she was such a joy to visit, had been married, but her spouse had been deceased for many years. She never had children of her own. After her spouse died and Joy became unable to live alone, her great-niece had moved her from up north to live with her and her family. She had been with them for many years. The deep love they had for one another was evident as I observed and listened to them share memories of the good times they had enjoyed together.

As I visited over the next couple of months, I learned that Joy's favorite chair had been placed next to the sliding glass door so she could enjoy the kids playing in the pool in the backyard, watch the birds, and observe the changing of the seasons. I also discovered that she had a stash of goodies hidden on the far side of her chair. This stash included chocolate candy, cookies, and soft peppermints. Once I realized how much she enjoyed soft peppermints, I tried to make sure she always had a fresh supply. She was very protective of her stash of goodies, because never once did she offer me any.

We always had such wonderful visits, with a lot of laughter and the sharing of memories. She would ask about my family, and I would encourage her to share about hers. She spoke often of her deceased spouse and the life they had lived together. One day, with a faraway look in her eyes, she told me that her greatest regret in life was never having had a child of her own. Finally, with a smile on her face, she told me that her great-niece's children had become like her own. She was living with the family when the youngest son was born, and she told me more than once what a great blessing it had been when she got to hold him in her arms just after he was born. I could tell this was one of the highlights of her life. Later, as she approached her last days, she also shared with me that her only concern about dying was the effect it would have on the youngest child. He had never known a time when she wasn't present for him. Even though he was ten years of age, she was concerned about how he would cope with her death.

On one visit, I asked Joy if there was anything she didn't get to do in her 101 years of life that she wished she had. She told me that she had never learned to swim. I pointed to the pool in the backyard and told her there was still time. Her family could take her to the pool and teach her to swim. Without missing a beat, she turned to me and said, "Chaplain, I wouldn't look good in a bikini!"

I also asked Joy what she considered to be the greatest thing she had ever seen in 101 years of life. She surprised me with her answer. She told me of a day when she and her sister had come home from school and her father had told them to turn off the oil lamps they used for light in the house. She and her sister objected, telling their father it would be dark. He insisted again that they turn off the lamps, and they did as he had instructed. Once the oil lamps were out, and they were standing in the dark, she and her sister heard a clicking sound. Suddenly there was light. With awe, they saw a single electric bulb hanging over their heads. This, she said, was the most amazing thing she had seen in her many years of life.

Over the next few months as I visited with Joy, I could see the sparkle slowly leaving her eyes, and I knew she was approaching her last days. Finally, she told me that she was tired and ready to go to home. When I asked what she meant by this, she told me she was ready to die and go to heaven. She just couldn't understand why God would leave her on earth for so long when she was so weary and so ready to go.

Joy was still with her family when her 102nd birthday came, and I had the privilege of attending her party. She had looked forward to it with anticipation, but I could tell that all the guests and festivities were overwhelming and tiring for her. I only stayed for a few minutes, but before leaving, I congratulated her once again. I also told her I would dance at her 105th birthday party. She still hadn't lost her sense of humor, and she laughed and told me I would be too old!

One day not long after her party, I received a call from her nurse, telling me Joy had become unresponsive. If I wanted to see her one more time, I should probably go right away. When I arrived at the great-niece's home, the family had gathered at Joy's bedside. They parted enough to allow me to get up to the bed where I took her hand, leaned over, and spoke quietly into her ear. I assured her of God's love. I also told her that I loved her and would see her again one day on the other side. Even though she had been totally unresponsive up to that point, Joy squeezed my hand, letting me know she had heard and that she loved me too. I stayed for a while, encouraging the family to share memories and laughter, because that is what Joy would want. She would want to know all was well with her loved ones when the angels came to escort her home.

Joy went home a day later with her family at her side. She had heard her family's laughter in the midst of their tears. I feel confident that their presence and their laughter brought her great comfort until the angels arrived, and then she heard the glorious singing of the heavenly chorus as she was welcomed home. As I reflected on the months I had the blessing of Joy in my life, one of the things that stood out was her beauty. Even though her skin was wrinkled and her body frail, she was beautiful. It wasn't her outward appearance that made her beautiful but her sweet, gentle spirit. I also realized I had learned so much from her in those few short months. She shared the wisdom and knowledge with me that came from 102 years of life experience. I can only hope that I will be able to pass on to others what I had learned from her. I think God would like that, and I know Joy would be pleased.

LIFE LESSON

Someone has said that beauty is in the eye of the beholder, and I'm sure there is some truth in that. However, I think we often miss true beauty, such as Joy's, because we have mistakenly accepted the world's definition of it. God gives us the best definition, the one that certainly describes

Joy and so many other people whose beauty the world's standard would find falling short of its requirements.

> Your beauty should not come from outward adornment, such as braided hair and the wearing of gold jewelry and fine clothes. Instead, it should be that of your inner self, the unfading beauty of a gentle and quiet spirit, which is of great worth in God's sight. (1 Peter 3:3–4)

REFLECTIONS

CHAPTER 6

God Still Speaks

Phil and Marian lived in a beautiful home in an affluent gated community, but they were very humble, giving God the praise and thanksgiving for all the blessings He had brought into their lives. They had been very active in their church until the patient's Alzheimer's disease had advanced too far for them to attend. Fortunately, their pastor and church family had faithfully continued to minister to them in wonderful ways. Despite the spiritual support they were already receiving, their hospice nurse encouraged Marian to accept visits from the hospice chaplain. She agreed, and this was the beginning of a remarkable story.

Most of my first visit was spent in the sunroom talking with Marian while Phil slept, something he was doing more often as his disease progressed. Marian became tearful at times as she spoke of their many happy years together. The thoughts of losing her husband were painful, but the reality of watching him linger and suffer was even worse. The situation had become even more difficult recently since Phil had become fearful and easily agitated. He didn't want Marian to leave his sight, and she was weary and worn by her constant caregiver duties.

I discovered over the next few visits that Marian was not one to complain. Despite the stress and strain of all she was going through, she told me she considered it a privilege to be able to care for her husband who had taken such good care of her for so many years. She laughed as she related an incident that had occurred just before he became so confused. He had wakened one morning and insisted they go to the local Cadillac dealership. He wanted to buy her a new car. He insisted that she needed a safe and reliable car that would last many years after he was gone. She had tried her best to talk him out of spending the money, but he was not to be denied. And that is how she came to own the shiny new Cadillac SUV sitting in their garage.

Phil declined rapidly, and a few weeks later, he was admitted to the inpatient unit. I visited with Marian and Phil regularly, but he had already fallen into a coma. Their daughter had arrived from out of town, and Marian was finding comfort from her presence. They both were finding strength from God and the ongoing support of their church family.

Very early one morning, after Phil had been in the inpatient unit for several days, I was wakened from a sound sleep. Phil's name was the first thing that came to my mind. I felt sure God had wakened me for a reason. Suddenly, I felt as if the Holy Spirit was telling me that Phil was going to die that morning, and I needed to get up, get ready, and go to the inpatient unit to be with his family. Without any doubt as to what was happening, or from whom I was receiving my directions, I did as He instructed. My wife asked why I was up so early. An early morning call often indicated an emergency, but she hadn't heard the phone ring. I quickly explained that God had wakened me and told me one of our patients was about to die. I needed to be present with the family.

Interestingly enough, I didn't feel rushed. I felt an assurance that I would arrive on time, according to God's schedule. In fact, I was so confident of this that I went through the twenty-four-hour McDonald's drive-through just across the highway from the inpatient unit and picked up a biscuit and a cup of coffee.

I arrived at the inpatient unit sometime between 4:30 and 5:00 a.m. As I had expected, I saw Marian's new Cadillac in the parking lot. I knew she had been called in by one of the staff. The entrance door was always locked at night for security purposes, and it was so early in the morning that it had not yet been opened. I had to call inside to the nurse's station to have someone unlock the door. When the nurse opened the door, she told me she was glad I had come, because the patient in room ten was actively dying. I told her I knew, and she looked at me strangely and asked how I knew. I told her it was a God thing. I took my briefcase, biscuit, and coffee to my office. I then walked down the hall to Phil's room, knowing what I would probably find when I arrived.

Marian and her daughter were at Phil's bedside, holding his hands. Marian looked at me with surprise. She told me that she thought Phil was about to go. I shook my head in acknowledgment and asked if I could pray. They readily agreed, and as Phil's wife and daughter quietly wept, I placed my hand on his head and began to pray. I had just begun when I realized Phil's spirit had just departed. He was no longer present with us. Marian also recognized that Phil's long struggle was finally over.

The nurse came in to pronounce him, and I held Marian as she sobbed. Finally, as the tears began to slow, Marian looked up at me and asked how I knew to come. I told her that God had wakened me and told me it was time. She thanked me for listening to God and being there for them.

When I told other staff members what had happened that morning, some began to share their own stories of how God had spoken to them so clearly they had no doubt as to whom they were hearing. As I reflected on the events of that day, I was in awe of the fact that God would wake me so early in the morning and lead me to be right where He wanted me to be at just the time He wanted me to be there. But then, why should I be surprised? He's God and He never sleeps!

LIFE LESSON

It has been my experience that God seldom shouts, but He often speaks in a whisper. Sometimes it's in the silence of the night. Maybe that's the only time we are quiet enough and free from the deafening sounds of the world, enabling us to hear Him. My wife tells me that God often speaks to me at 2:00 or 3:00 in the morning, because it's the only time I'm not talking. As much as I hate to admit it, she's probably right. Maybe we should all seek silence instead of constantly running from it. Turn off the TV and the radio, and find a solitary and quiet place—and listen. God has some mighty interesting things to say. Can you hear Him now?

The Lord said, "Go out and stand on the mountain in the presence of the Lord, for the Lord is about to pass by." Then a great and powerful wind tore the mountains apart and shattered the rocks before the Lord, but the Lord was not in the wind. After the wind there was an earthquake, but the Lord was not in the earthquake. After the earthquake came a fire, but the Lord was not in the fire. And after the fire came a gentle whisper. (1 Kings 19:11–12)

REFLECTIONS

CHAPTER 7

Love in the Midst of Differences

When Sandy arrived at the inpatient unit, all I really knew about her was that she was unresponsive, and her family had not yet arrived. When I went to her room, I noticed several women had come to see her, and they were all gathered around her bed. As I entered her room and introduced myself, I felt a certain amount of suspicion and even hostility from some of them. They quickly informed me they were all Sandy's friends, and they wanted to be left alone with her. I asked them to let us know if they needed anything, and as gracefully as I could, I left the room.

I shared my experience with the patient's nurse, and she informed me that the patient was gay and those were her friends. I then understood why they might be a little leery of having a chaplain visit, possibly having had some bad experiences with "religious" people. Later, Sandy's father and stepmother arrived, and I offered to minister to them in any way I could. They were obviously distraught over their daughter's impending death but were appreciative of the care she was receiving from the hospice staff. I continued in my visits with other patients and thought nothing more of the encounters.

The next morning, Sandy's nurse came to me and asked for my assistance. It seemed that Sandy's father and stepmother were very upset that her friends were staying with her round the clock. This made it impossible for them to visit privately with their daughter. They had asked the friends to leave but had met open hostility. Sandy's friends began to vent their anger toward her father, accusing him of rejecting his daughter and her lifestyle for years. From their perspective, he had

38

no business trying to show his love and acceptance of her now that she was dying.

The nurse and the aide had asked all of them to leave Sandy's room so they could bathe her. They were all now sitting in one of the family rooms. No one was speaking, and the tension in the room was palpable. The nurse was very afraid things were about to get uglier, and she asked if I would intervene.

As I began to walk down the hall toward the family room, I prayed diligently. I had no idea what I could say or do to try to diffuse what sounded like a very volatile situation. I knew it was only the Holy Spirit who could intervene and bring peace in situations such as this. Boy, did I need Him then.

When I turned the corner into the family room, I found the situation to be just as the nurse had described it. The patient's father and stepmother were sitting on a couch on one side of the room, and her friends were sitting in the other chairs across from them. Not a word was being spoken, and none needed to be. The looks on their faces said it all. Anger and hostility were all that I saw.

But God (there's that phrase again) is good. And it was as if the Holy Spirit took control before I ever opened my mouth. I introduced myself to everyone once again, because I saw some new faces. Without waiting for any response, I said that Sandy must be very special and greatly loved to have so many people present with her. I then asked them to tell me about Sandy, what it was they loved so much about her. It was as if a floodgate had been opened. Her friends began to share memories and talk of Sandy's love and compassion for others. As they shared and laughed in the midst of their tears, I could feel the tension begin to leave the room. After listening to some of her friends, Sandy's father began to share memories of his "little girl" as tears ran down his face. Soon, rather than anger and hostility, there was a feeling of peace and closeness that a few minutes before would have seemed impossible.

As silence slowly entered the room once again, I asked if everyone would be agreeable to my offering a prayer. After a moment of hesitation, everyone shook their heads yes. Taking another step of faith, I asked everyone to stand, form a circle, and hold hands, showing our unity and oneness in our love for Sandy. At first I thought this was more than they were willing to do, but thankfully, everyone joined hands, and the circle was closed. I couldn't help but notice Sandy's father and stepmother holding hands with those, who only minutes ago, had seemed to be their worst enemies. In the quietness of the moment, as I began to pray, a wonderful sense of Jesus's presence settled over the room. When I finished, there were hugs all around.

At my suggestion, we all crossed the hall and entered Sandy's room, where we formed another circle around her bed. I again offered a prayer. I felt confident Sandy had heard our prayer, and I hoped it had brought some peace and comfort to her. I was confident that having her family and friends gathered around her most certainly did. The unity of those who loved her, friends and family alike, was a wonderful thing to see. As I left the room, I knew I had just seen God perform another healing miracle.

Sandy died the very next day, and I met her father and stepmother in the hall as they were leaving. Her father hugged me and thanked me for helping him to overcome his anger and prejudice so that he could enjoy his final hours with his daughter. I pointed up and reminded him that God gets all the praise and glory.

LIFE LESSON

There is something so cleansing and freeing about forgiveness. It's really not for the person we are forgiving. It's for us. It sets us free from sleepless nights and anxiety-filled days. Forgiveness is noble. Forgiveness is acting like Jesus, and it is what God does for us, even though we don't deserve it.

> Bear with each other and forgive whatever grievances you may have against one another. Forgive as the Lord forgave you. And over all these virtues put on love, which binds them all together in perfect unity. (Colossians 3:13–14)

REFLECTIONS

CHAPTER 8

A Divine Appointment

I believe in divine appointments. My definition of a divine appointment is God orchestrating events so that two or more people come together at a specific time and place so that His plan and purpose can be fulfilled. I have encountered too many of them over the years to dismiss them as coincidences. After all, someone has said that a coincidence is simply God at work without taking credit for what has taken place.

I had gone to my office at the inpatient unit very early one morning to catch up on some charting and reports. I found I could accomplish a great deal in the quietness of that time, before the busyness of the day began. My office at the inpatient unit was right next to the small but intimate and comfortable chapel. As I was working on a report, I realized I would have to go to the nurse's station to get some additional information to finish it. Coming out of my office door, I almost ran into a man who apparently was just coming out of the chapel. We both stepped back, looked at each other, and said, "I'm sorry," almost at the same time. Then we really looked at each other. I am sure we were both thinking the same thing. What a contrast. Here I stood with my suit and tie, my daily uniform, and there he stood in his biker's outfit, complete with a leather vest, boots, tattoos, and ponytail. I guessed he had just ridden in on his Harley, and I later learned that I wasn't far off the mark. I don't know why, but the thought went through my mind that I wish someone could get a picture of this.

As I looked at his face, I could see pain in his eyes and tears that would soon start falling. I asked if I could help him, and he told me his mother was a new patient there. He had just been in the chapel trying to pray, but he wasn't sure how to pray. He doubted if God even heard his prayers. I asked if he would like to return to the chapel with me so we could talk privately. He readily agreed, and I discerned that God had brought me in early that morning because He had a divine appointment for the two of us.

As he sat on the front pew of the chapel, and I sat in a chair facing him, he began to tell me his story. He lived out of state and had come to be with his mother until she died. He loved her greatly, and he shared memories of what a good and loving mother she had been. He was heartbroken that he had not always been present for her. He had lived a lifestyle that he was sure had caused her a lot of grief and tears. His mother was a godly woman, and he knew she had been praying for him for years. Now she was unresponsive, and he couldn't tell her how much he loved her and how sorry he was for not always being the son she deserved. His confession came with tears of regret.

When the words and tears finally came to a stop, I assured him his mother could still hear him. I wanted him to know there was still time to tell her what was in his heart. While this appeared to give him some comfort, I could tell something was still burdening him. I asked him if there was something else he wanted to talk about. He looked at me as if he was surprised, and then asked how I knew. With a smile, I replied that God sometimes had a way of making those things known to us. If he wanted to tell me the rest of the story, I was willing to listen.

The tears started once again as he told me how God had been speaking to his heart. He knew his mother had prayed for his salvation for many years, but as he sat in the chapel earlier, it was almost as if God had spoken to Him in an audible voice and told him it was time. He wasn't sure if he was really hearing from God, or if God could even forgive and accept him after all the things he had done in his life. I assured him of God's unconditional love. He listened closely as I spoke of the mercy, grace, and forgiveness God extends to those who come to His Son, Jesus, in faith, with repentant hearts. He expressed his desire to do this, but he wasn't sure how. As the two of us sat in that little chapel in the early morning stillness, I helped him make his profession of faith in Jesus. I listened as he prayed, asking Jesus to forgive him of his sins, to be His Lord and Savior, and to give him eternal life.

When he had finished praying, I prayed for him while holding his hands, and then both of us stood and embraced as tears ran down both of our faces. I couldn't help but think what a picture we would have made: the chaplain and the biker hugging and crying tears of joy! In my own heart, I was silently thanking the Lord for bringing me in early that morning for this divine appointment and for allowing me to experience the miracle of seeing another soul saved.

I told him how excited I was about his decision. I assured him I would be praying for him as he began this new journey in his life as a child of God. I thought this was the end of the story, but I soon found this wasn't the case. He told me that he wanted to go to his mother's room and tell her that her prayers had been answered. All her prayers for his salvation had finally come to fruition. I said I thought that would be wonderful. I reminded him that she would be able to hear him. I felt confident his words would bring her joy and comfort even if she may not be able to respond to him verbally.

I noticed that he hesitated for a minute. I asked him if something was wrong or if there was something else he wanted to talk about. It was then this rugged-looking biker asked if I would go with him to talk with his mother. He didn't want to be alone, and he wasn't sure if he would have the right words to say. I assured Tim that I would consider it a privilege to be there with him. I also assured him that God would give him the words to say. I could see relief come over his face, and his whole body relaxed for the first time that morning.

As we walked down the hall toward his mother's room, I placed my hand on his shoulder and silently prayed for what was about to take place. I couldn't help but be reminded of the story of the prodigal son found in Luke 15:11–32. A wayward son was about to express his deep love for his dying mother, and a praying mother was about to hear the most wonderful words a son could ever share with her. When we arrived in her room, sunrise was just casting its glow across her bed. She lay silently and peacefully, her breathing very shallow.

As her son approached his mother's bed, he reached over and took my hand for moral support. As he began to talk, tears began to fall from his eyes onto his mother's face. He told her he loved her and that her prayers had been answered. He had just given his heart to Jesus. He then bent over and kissed her cheek as he wiped his tears from her face. And then his mother, who had been totally unresponsive up to that time, blessed her son with a beautiful smile as affirmation she had heard him. As I observed this touching scene, I was overwhelmed by a sense of the Lord's presence in the room. All I could do was to silently thank Him again for allowing me the privilege of being a part of this divine appointment and the miracle that had unfolded before my eyes. After a few moments of silence, I prayed with the patient and her son, and when I had finished, he turned and gave me a bear hug that almost squeezed the breath out of my body.

Over the years I have had the privilege many times of introducing people to Jesus and hearing them make a profession of faith, but I have never seen anyone who was more excited than my biker friend. While we were still standing beside his mother's bed, the nurse and an aide walked in, and he couldn't wait to tell them he had just been saved. In fact, he told everyone he encountered at the inpatient unit, including staff members, family members, and even strangers. When he ran out of people there to tell the good news to, he got on his cell phone and started calling others. He was what I would call "radically saved!"

Two days later, his dear sweet mother went very peacefully to be with the Lord. I could only think of how wonderful it was that she was able to experience the joy of knowing her prayers for her son had been answered. How exciting it was that she would see him again one day in heaven. Her son? No longer was he burdened with regrets, but he was rejoicing that his mother was safely home. His tears were tears of grief now mixed with tears of joy. Thank You, Father, for divine appointments.

LIFE LESSON

Sometimes God answers prayers quickly, but at other times, He answers them after they have been repeated many times, over many years. Sometimes we have the joy of seeing them answered, but many of our prayers may not be answered in our lifetime. However, God always answers the prayers of His children in His time and in His way. For a dying patient or a grieving family, prayer is often like a comforting salve. Prayer invites God into the circumstances to provide the comfort and peace only He can give. This is why the apostle Paul was able to write,

> Do not be anxious about anything, but in everything, by prayer and petition, with thanksgiving, present your requests to God. And the peace of God, which transcends all understanding, will guard your hearts and your minds in Christ Jesus. (Philippians 4:6–7)

Who knows? Maybe your prayers will result in a divine appointment.

REFLECTIONS

CHAPTER 9

The Different Languages of Love

It all started one day when I received a phone call from a nurse who worked in the other chaplain's territory. It just so happened that she was one of my favorite nurses, and we had worked several very difficult, but rewarding, cases together. She asked if I would be willing to take on a new case in her territory, because the patient had requested a male chaplain. The chaplain assigned to this case originally is female.

In addition, the patient was going to be quite a challenge for everyone involved, and she knew how much I enjoyed a good challenge. Knowing that the nurse was always very honest and very discerning in her assessments, I agreed to accept the case with the other chaplain's approval, which I did receive.

On my first visit to the patient's home, I soon realized this was a unique situation. Both the patient, Fred, and his wife, Gladys, were in their nineties. They still lived in their home, but they did have a daughter and a son-in-law who checked on them each day, bought their groceries, and took care of any other needs they might have. Obviously it was a very stressful situation for the daughter and her husband, because they were in their sixties and had been doing this for a number of years. They were extremely tired, and I soon recognized that her parents were not ones to express their gratitude.

Fred and Gladys lived in a nice brick home in a well-kept neighborhood. When I arrived at their house, I rang the doorbell and waited. Nothing happened, and I didn't hear anything, but I felt sure they wouldn't have gone anywhere. So I rang the doorbell again, and someone finally came, opened the door, and told me to come in. The gentleman didn't even ask who I was as he turned his back and started up the steps of the split-level home. We were going toward what I soon learned was the den.

My first thoughts were that this could not be the patient who was walking up the steps. The patient was in his nineties, and he surely wasn't able to do that. I also thought that this was not a very safe home for people in their nineties, with all the steps they would have to navigate. I soon saw that the main living quarters, with the den, kitchen, and bedrooms, were all on the same level. Fortunately, the couple didn't have to deal with the steps that often. The only reason the man had to come down the steps to open the door for me was because the patient's daughter had not yet arrived.

I quickly found that the man who had come down the steps and opened the door was none other than the patient. He curtly told me he had yelled for me to come around to the back door, but I didn't listen to him and follow his directions, so he had to come down the steps and open the door for me. I felt like a child who had just been reprimanded for my failure to follow simple instructions. We were off to a good start.

Fred sat on the couch, patted the seat next to him, and told me to sit. Once again I failed to follow instructions. I saw an elderly lady sitting in a chair next to the couch, and I assumed this must be his wife. So before sitting down, I went to her, offered my hand, and introduced myself. She had a very sour look on her face, and I took this to mean she might not be glad to meet me. I later learned to not take it personally, because that was her normal facial expression. Then I made a fatal mistake. I asked her how she was doing, and by the time she was finished telling me, I felt as if she should be the hospice patient rather than her husband.

Once that unpleasantness was over, I sat on the couch next to Fred, who by this time appeared to be completely put out with me. I think he had already formed the opinion that I was a complete dunce who was incapable of following the simplest of instructions. It was then that Gladys made a very slow exit from the room, indicating that she had nothing to contribute to our conversation. She never even said it was nice to meet me, goodbye, or she hoped I didn't come back. I wasn't sure how I might have offended her in such a short time but decided I would have to sort that out later.

Fred informed me that he was hard of hearing, and that was why he wanted me to sit right next to him on the couch. After all, there is nothing like getting to know someone better than by being up close and personal. Here we were on this very large couch, sitting next to each other in the middle, like two love birds on a fence. Fred seemed very dour at first, and he reminded me of the man holding the pitchfork in the Grant Wood painting titled *American Gothic*. As we got to know each other better, I told him one day that he was a Midwestern stoic who somehow took a wrong turn and ended up in the south. That almost got a smile out of him. At least I thought that's what it was.

Our first visit was a little strained, and I felt as if I was being interviewed for a job. I later learned that was exactly what it was. He was testing me, checking me out to see if he wanted me to come back for future visits. His first concern seemed to be my religious beliefs, which I had no problem sharing with him. Then he started delving into my political leanings, and this was an area of conversation I always tried to avoid with patients, for obvious reasons. It became clear that we would have to have that conversation whether I wanted to or not if the visit was to continue. I was very relieved when I found that we agreed on most things, and these two topics became the basis for our future conversation.

I must have passed Fred's test, because he invited me to come back. In fact, he wanted to know how often I could come. I explained that my schedule would only allow me one visit per month, and he seemed a little disappointed, but he accepted this for the time being. I also learned very quickly that each of my visits with Fred would last a minimum of one to two hours. Because of my heavy caseload, I would try to keep my home patient visits to no more than fifteen to thirty minutes, but getting away from Fred proved to be a challenge. If I said I had to go and he didn't feel the visit had been long enough, he would pout and ask why I was in such a hurry. He even resorted to the old guilt trip one day by telling me it might be our last visit because he could die before I returned.

It wasn't long before our visits fell into a comfortable routine. His daughter would let me in the house when I arrived. She would go into the kitchen that was open to the den and act as if she was busy cleaning. I could tell though that she was listening to our conversation, because every once in a while she would interject her own thoughts or opinions. It really wasn't much of a challenge for her to hear us when you consider that I had to yell so Fred could hear me. As I said earlier, our topics were pretty much limited to two areas: religion and politics.

Another routine in our visits was Gladys slowly getting out of her chair and leaving the room, often without saying a word. One day she surprised me. She walked slowly by Fred and me sitting on the couch and said, "You old fool. All you do is watch the news every night and fuss about it." I never did decide if she was talking about me or Fred!

I never had to do much preparation for my visits with Fred, because our conversations were the same every time. He would say the same things, almost as if he had memorized them, and I would normally respond in the same way so as not to disrupt our routine. Visiting Fred often reminded me of the movie *Groundhog Day* in which a man kept living the same day over and over.

As the months passed, I became more and more fond of Fred, and he became more comfortable with me. He slowly began to open up and share a little bit about his childhood. He spoke of how he had always been a loner and just never felt that he fit in with the other kids. This feeling continued on into his adulthood. He seemed to become sad when he talked about this. He spoke of the jobs he had over the years and how he and Gladys met and married. I could sense that Fred was sometimes lost in these memories, and it was almost as if I was no longer sitting next to him.

In looking back, I also believe Fred knew his time was short, and he felt a need to tell someone his story, someone who would just listen without judgment. His children and his wife no longer wanted to hear the same stories he had been telling them for years. With me, he had a new audience, one who would not say, "You've told me that story before."

One day, as he and I were standing next to each other, looking out the front window, Fred said, "Chaplain, some days I stand and look out the window at people going by, and I just wish someone would stop and talk with me." I said, "Fred, you have your wife here to talk with every day." Fred looked at me as if I had lost my mind and replied, "Chaplain, we have been married over seventy years. We've pretty much said everything to each other we have to say." This is still one of my fondest memories.

Speaking of marriage, one day Fred told me he and Gladys had been married seventy-two years. Gladys overheard this and told me they had been married seventy years. Like a child, Fred said, "Seventy-two years." To which Gladys replied, "It doesn't matter. It seems like an eternity." Ah, the many languages of love.

I asked Fred one day if he knew for sure he would go to heaven when he died. He responded that he was. He pointed down the hall and said that he had settled that matter one morning on his knees in his bedroom. He was just a young man then, in his seventies! Fred believed that God was energy, we were just a small part of that energy, and when we died, we would return to the source of it all.

He eventually became too weak to stay at home. He was moved to our inpatient unit where he eventually passed away. Gladys was heartbroken and completely lost without him. She followed him a few months later. Did she die of a broken heart as some said? I don't know the answer to that question, but what I do know is that they stayed together for seventy years or more, and there had to be a lot of love involved for that to happen.

In all the months I visited with Fred, I never heard him or Gladys say any words of endearment to each other. Most of their conversation was what I called "sniping" at each other. I've seen this type of behavior many times when in the presence of couples who have been married for many years. What I have learned, after observing most of them, is that this was their way of communicating, of expressing their love for one another. It may not have been my way or yours, but it was theirs, because you see, it is just one of the many different languages of love.

LIFE LESSON

Have you ever thought about how you and your spouse or significant other communicate? If you pay attention to it, you might be surprised.

I would also encourage you to keep your ears open to it as the years go by, because I have noted in my own marriage that our love language has continued to evolve into a quite different form of communication. You may have been noticing this in your relationships too. This is okay as long as it continues to be a language of love.

> And now these three remain: faith, hope, and love. But the greatest of these is love. (1 Corinthians 13:13)

REFLECTIONS

CHAPTER 10

Her Witness Lives On

Her name was Deborah. She sat silently by her mother's bedside for hours each day in the inpatient unit. For many of those who sit vigilantly at a dying loved one's bedside, it can be a very lonely time, especially if they don't have a good support system from friends and other family members. It can also be a time of reflection, recalling good memories that can bring a smile to a face and comfort to a hurting heart in the midst of difficult circumstances. For others, it can be a time in which old hurts are recalled and old wounds are reopened, resulting in feelings of anger, animosity, and often regret. For Deborah, as I found through the hours I spent with her, these silent times alone with her mother were a combination of all these things.

I would often find her reading her Bible or a Christian-based book. Deborah was a woman of deep faith, a faith she had learned from her godly mother who was soon to see the Savior she loved face-to-face. I had many long conversations with Deborah during the days her mother lingered so near to death's door. We talked about everything, from her childhood experiences to biblical truths. She spoke of how her mother lived out her faith, and as a result, many people had come to know the Lord.

But after a few days, Deborah's conversation began to turn more and more to why God had not yet taken her mother home. Her mother had been such a good and faithful servant, why would God allow her to suffer in her present condition? Deborah knew that her mother was so ready to go be with Him and her loved ones who were there waiting for her. As I had told so many people in the past who had the same question about a loved one, God is the only one who knows the answer to that question. We have no choice but to trust that He has a perfect plan and purpose for all that He does. Over the years, I had also discerned from my observations that God sometimes used the loved one's lingering to work in the life of those who are going to be left behind.

I could tell that the long hours of waiting were severely testing Deborah's faith as well as her physical and emotional endurance. As so many people do during these times of waiting, she had gone from shock and sadness that she was about to lose her mother to anxiety as to why her mother would not "let go." Then came the anger with God for not taking her quickly. In the midst of these emotional changes, she, like so many others, was often overcome with guilt about having these feelings. I explained to her that these feelings were normal, and it didn't mean she was a bad person, just a hurting person. I reinforced to her that God loved her and her mother, that He was present with them every minute of every day, and that He understood all her feelings.

Finally, Deborah's mother passed in the early morning hours when neither Deborah nor I was present. I received the news the next morning when I returned to the inpatient unit. I attempted to call Deborah to express my condolences, but no one answered the phone. I left a brief message, assuring her of my continued prayers. I had not discussed the details of her mother's funeral arrangements with Deborah, but she had indicated that she had a pastor who would officiate at the service when the time came. I thought no more about it and was soon lost in the daily and very busy routine of a chaplain's life.

I was surprised when I received a call from Deborah a few days later, asking if I would share a few words at her mother's service. She gave me the details of the day, time, and location, and after checking my schedule, I assured her I would be available. I asked if another minister would be participating, and she told me the pastor friend she had mentioned before would be speaking as well. I told her I was honored she had asked me to participate, and I would see her the day of the service. I later received a call from an employee of the funeral home where the service was to be held. He wanted to confirm that I was participating in the service. It was then I learned there would actually be three speakers, including me.

I called Deborah the day before the service to ask if there were any particular verses of scripture or any special memories she wanted me to share. She then explained to me that a lay minister she and her mother had known for many years would give the eulogy. Her pastor friend would read some scripture and share a message. On hearing this, I was confused about my part in the service, and I expressed my concern to Deborah. I was very surprised and very humbled by her explanation.

Deborah felt certain there would be people at the service who didn't know Jesus. In fact, her brother and sister-in-law would be there, and she and her mother had been praying for their salvation for many years. Deborah wanted to have the plan of salvation presented at her mother's service, followed by an invitation for people to respond. She knew this would be what her mother would want. Deborah also felt that nothing would please her mother, or honor her life and death, more than people being saved at her funeral. She had spoken with the other two ministers, and neither of them felt comfortable presenting the plan of salvation at a funeral. After having spent so much time talking with me at her mother's bedside, she knew my heart and my burden for the lost. She wanted me to be the one to present the plan of salvation and offer the invitation. She also asked that I begin praying for her family members and any others who might be present who needed the Lord.

As I was driving to the funeral home the next day, I was so overcome with emotion that I had to pull off the side of the road. Tears began to flow. I have always been in awe of the fact that God could use me as His tool to minister to others in His name. It is a very humbling thought. That morning, I was also feeling overwhelmed in the confidence Deborah had placed in me and the hope that she had for those who would be in attendance at the service. So sitting on the side of the road about one mile from the funeral home, I poured out my heart to the Lord, surrendering myself to Him, to be used however He saw fit. I asked for Him to do something so big there could be no doubt it was His hand at work through the power of His Holy Spirit. I thanked Him in advance for what He was about to do.

When I pulled into the parking lot of the funeral home and started to get out of my car, I looked into the rearview mirror and saw that my eyes were red and puffy from crying. I couldn't help but wonder what people would think, but I also felt the comfort and confidence that God's Holy Spirit was with me. He would guide my every word. Before the service began, I met with the other two speakers, and we determined an order of service. The lay minister would give the eulogy first, followed by the other pastor, with me coming last.

As the service began and the three of us sat on the platform facing the family members and friends in attendance, I felt the abiding, calming presence of the Holy Spirit as I prayed. The eulogy was short but very touching. The other pastor only read one passage of scripture, closed his Bible, said a prayer, and then sat down. After a song, I stood to present the Good News of salvation through faith in Jesus Christ. I looked at Deborah sitting on the front pew with her family, and she barely nodded her head and smiled.

I wish I could take credit for what took place after that, but I have to give all the credit to God. Seven people were saved that day, including Deborah's family members she and her mother had prayed for so many times!

As I walked out of the chapel that morning, Deborah gave me a big hug. With tears running down her face, she said her prayers and those of her mother had been answered. I couldn't help but think that her mother had been looking down on the service, and there was a big celebration going on in heaven. How amazing that God had used not only her mother's life but her death as well to bring such a great blessing to so many others. Even after death, her witness lives on.

LIFE LESSON

Many people think life ends when we die. Nothing could be further from the truth. From a spiritual perspective, the soul departs from the body at the time of death, and it continues to live. From an earthly perspective, our lives continue on in the memories of others. As we have just seen, our prayers and our witness are still viable, even after our lives have ended on earth. Heaven doesn't forget them. Our witness still has power after we are gone because of the power of a loving, omniscient, and omnipotent God. So pray as if other people's lives depend on it, because they might. Let your life be a witness of your faith—a witness that has eternal consequences and ongoing influence.

The prayer of a righteous man is powerful and effective. (James 5:16)

REFLECTIONS

CHAPTER 11

The Sacrifices of Love

Sometimes my visits to newly admitted home patients served to bring back many memories. One morning, as I was looking at the list of those patients in my territory, I noticed that one of them lived in the neighborhood where I had bought my very first home. That had been over forty years ago, and I was anxious to see what the old neighborhood looked like after all those years.

As I pulled into the subdivision for my first meeting with the patient and her family, it was somewhat of a disappointment when I saw my old home. The years had taken a toll on the area, and the homes were nothing like I had remembered them. When I arrived at the patient's home, however, I was pleasantly surprised to see that it was well maintained, almost like an oasis in the middle of a desert.

When I knocked on the front door, I was met by a very pleasant middle-aged woman who told me she was the patient's daughter. She invited me in and introduced me to her father, who was sitting in a recliner in the living room of the small house. He had a TV tray next to his chair, and he appeared to have everything he needed close at hand. A walker also stood next to the chair. The daughter asked me to visit with her father while she finished bathing her mother. The patient's husband was a very friendly but reserved man who at first was slow to open up to me. As I visited with him and his family over the next few weeks, he began to openly share his feelings about their circumstances.

The patient and her husband had been married over fifty years. There was no doubt as he spoke about her that he loved her dearly and watching her suffer and decline so slowly was taking a toll on him as well as their children. He also revealed that he was on dialysis and his son or daughter would have to take him to his treatments several times a week. This placed an additional burden on them. His son, who still worked, lived downstairs in the basement. His daughter and her family lived in Alabama, but she had been staying with her parents the majority of the time, only going home every other weekend. The son would take care of their parents when she was at home. I also learned that their daughter had been a nurse in the military and was well equipped to care for her mother.

One afternoon, while I was sitting with the patient's husband, I encouraged him to talk about his feelings, assuring him that what we discussed was strictly confidential. It was then he revealed to me that he was only taking dialysis so he could be with his wife until she passed away. As soon as she was gone, he would discontinue treatment, knowing that he would die soon after. He did not wish to live without her. He had discussed this with their children, and they had accepted his decision. He also asked me to pray that God would be merciful and take his wife home very soon.

During each visit, I would go to the back bedroom to visit with the patient after spending time with her husband. At times he would grab his walker and go with me, and at other times he was just too weak to do so. The patient's daughter was always present, and she would update me on all that had been taking place since I last visited with them. The patient always had a smile for me when I walked in, a smile that I often thought of as angelic. She had a sweet spirit and would allow me to hold her hand during our visits. She could not speak most of the time but would communicate with her eyes and a nod of her head. She enjoyed scripture and prayer, and I felt sure they both brought comfort to her. Even though she was completely bedridden and barely able to communicate, there was an aura of peace about her. I told her more than once that I wish I could bottle that and sell it, because I would become a millionaire.

The day after the patient died, I saw her daughter at the funeral home. The patient's husband was not present at the time. I often wonder if he did discontinue treatment as he had planned to do. My heart tells me that he did, because he wanted to be wherever the love of his life was. I also believe he wanted his daughter to go back to Alabama to be with her family. I am in awe of a love so great that it would lead a person to suffer along with another until the end.

LIFE LESSON

Most of us don't have any idea how we would respond if we were faced with circumstances like those of this dear couple. Altruistically, most of us want to believe we would remain faithful and be willing to make the same kind of sacrifice. Having seen this kind of love demonstrated many times over the years, I have come to understand that it is only possible when one remembers the vows made to each other and recognizes that love is not just a feeling but a commitment. We may not always feel like we are in love, but if we have already made the decision in our hearts to honor our commitment, no matter what the circumstances, we will not fail when difficulties come.

> To have and to hold from this day forward, for better or for worse, for richer, for poorer, in sickness and in health, to love and to cherish; till death us do part.
> —Traditional wedding vows

REFLECTIONS

CHAPTER 12

The Epitome of a Humble Heart

I arrived at the inpatient unit that morning prior to shift change, and one of the night nurses told me I just had to go see the patient in room seven as soon as possible. She described the patient as one of the sweetest people she had ever met, but she also warned me to be on top of my game spiritually. I wasn't quite sure what this meant. The nurse had walked off to finish her charting before shift change, and I didn't get a chance to discuss the subject any further. Her comment really stirred my curiosity, so as soon as I had checked my emails and voice mails, I went back to the nurse's station to take a look at room seven's chart.

From reading the chart, I found that the patient, Wilma, was a ninety-nine-year-old African American female who had been admitted the night before. Her diagnosis was failure to thrive, which simply meant she was no longer eating or drinking enough to sustain life for any long period of time. A son was listed as the next of kin. After reviewing the chart, I headed down the hall to room seven with a sense of anticipation that this could be an interesting visit.

I knocked on the door, and when I entered the room, I saw that the patient was alone. She appeared to be sleeping. She looked so small and frail, as if she would break if you hugged her too tightly. I decided to not disturb her and come back later after she had wakened, but as I turned to walk out the door, I heard a very soft voice say, "Come in. I'm awake."

I went to her bed and introduced myself as the chaplain. She gave me a most beautiful smile and thanked me for coming to see her. The first thought that came to my mind when I looked at her was the name

Jesus. Yes, I know that a ninety-nine-year-old frail and weak African American woman is not the picture most people would have of Jesus, but when I looked into her eyes, I just knew this was a woman who walked daily with Him. In fact, later in our visits I laughed and told her that Jesus just oozed out of her pores.

She reached out her skeletal hand to me, and as I took it, I had the sensation of touching leather, but I also felt a warmth and gentleness in it. As we began to talk, I found that her mind was sharp and clear. She had a very quick wit and a wonderful sense of humor. Her circumstances and her declining health were of no concern to her, because she was excited to be on her way to see Jesus. It also wasn't long before I understood the nurse's warning about being on top of my game spiritually. This dear sweet saint immediately wanted to hear my testimony concerning my salvation experience and my walk with the Lord. I felt like a student taking an oral exam before his teacher!

After we had talked a while, I told her I didn't want to wear out my welcome on the first visit, but I hoped she would let me come back and visit with her again. She insisted that I do that and asked that I bring my Bible next time and read some scripture to her. I assured her of this, and before I left the room, I held her hand and offered a prayer for her peace and comfort. I thanked God for the time we had together as brother and sister in Christ. Before I could let go of her hand, she pulled me down to her, hugged my neck, and planted a very gentle kiss on the side of my face. She then closed her eyes, and with a peaceful smile on her face, she appeared to drift off to sleep.

I found that I couldn't wait to see her each morning. I began to make it my routine to go to her room first, with my Bible. I would pick out different passages of scripture to read to her each day. I was amazed that as I was reading most of them, she was quoting them from memory. This lady was a living Bible if I had ever met one. As our relationship grew, we had some very deep spiritual conversations. I sometimes felt as if she could look right into my heart and soul. She was very discerning and very direct in her questions and comments. I soon realized I was the one being taught and ministered to.

She would occasionally have a visitor or two, but not as many as

I had expected. So one day I finally asked her if she had any children. With a faraway look in her eyes, and with a soft smile, she told me she had many children all over the world. When I asked how many, she replied that she wasn't sure. At first I thought that her illness and the medications were causing her to be confused, so I let the subject drop. One thing didn't change, however. Every day I would share scripture with her, and every day she would give me a hug and a kiss on the cheek. Some days after I had finished praying for her, she would hold onto my hand and pray for me. Each time her prayer seemed to open the door of heaven, and I had no doubt heaven was hearing with great delight.

One day as I entered her room, I saw she had company: a very tall young man whom she introduced as one of her sons. I shook his hand and spoke with him for just a moment. I told them I didn't want to interfere with their visit and would come back later. I met the young man in the hall not long after, and he shared a remarkable story with me. It seems that Wilma did have a lot of children all over the world. Her life had been dedicated to taking many children into her home, children who had no homes. Some were living in very difficult and even dangerous circumstances. She would love and nurture them as if they were her own, teaching them the Bible and instilling in them the importance of a good education.

The young man towering over me was a product of her kindness. She had raised him and assured that he had a good education. Later, he was able to go to college. He had earned his degree and now had a very successful career, all because of Wilma. He also told me that her one hundredth birthday was coming in a few days, and if she lived until then, he and many of her other "children" had planned a party for her in her room. Over the next couple of days, they would be arriving from all over the country to celebrate what would be her last birthday on earth and to thank her for what she had done for each of them. He warned me that we should expect a large crowd with a lot of laughter and a lot of tears. He graciously invited me to attend.

Just as he had predicted, on the day of Wilma's one hundredth birthday, people began arriving to celebrate with her. Each of them had their own story to share of how Wilma had been the primary influence for good in their lives. Someone had even put together a wonderful memory album with newspaper articles of Wilma's involvement in civic matters, letters and awards she had received, and memorabilia of the many other things she had accomplished throughout her life. I had been in the presence of a true celebrity without even knowing it. Wilma had never mentioned these things, because all she ever wanted to do was brag on Jesus. She truly was the epitome of a humble heart.

Even though by now she was extremely weak, and it was difficult for her to stay awake, it was obvious Wilma was overjoyed at having so many of her children surround her that day. After the cake had been eaten, the stories shared with laughter and tears as promised, and all her guests had left, I went to Wilma's room to check on her. She was so very weak now but still had that sweet, sweet smile. She was ready to go home—her heavenly home. I held her hand and prayed for a safe journey for her. I then leaned down to whisper in her ear that I would see her on the other side. I told her I loved her and kissed her on the cheek. The last words I ever heard her speak were "I love you too."

Wilma went home a couple of days later. It was a very sad morning when I arrived at the inpatient unit and was told she had completed her journey the night before. I was sad, but I was also rejoicing for her. Heaven was a much richer place, and earth was much poorer because she was gone, but one thing was certain. She had left her mark in the hearts of every person who encountered her, especially her many children all over the world. As I reflected on my visits with her and the way she had affected my life, I realized that while I may not have been spending time with Jesus in the flesh, I was pretty sure I had been with an angel.

LIFE LESSON

Yes, angels do exist. They come in many forms and in places we would not expect to meet with them. They often touch our lives in such subtle ways that we miss knowing who they are. At other times, their impact is so great we can't help but realize we have been visited by one. Why do I believe so strongly in their existence? First and foremost, I believe in the existence of angels because the Bible makes it clear they are real, created beings. Second, I believe they exist because I am quite certain I have met a few, and each encounter has had a life-changing impact on me. By the way, you don't have to go looking for them. They are all around you.

> Do not forget to entertain strangers, for by so doing some people have entertained angels without knowing it. (Hebrews 13:2)

REFLECTIONS

CHAPTER 13

The Greatest Treasure of All

Once again I was called on to accept a home patient who lived outside of my assigned territory. The patient was a female in her fifties who had been diagnosed with cancer. The doctors had done all they could for her, and now she was home, taking her final journey toward eternity. Her husband was a doctor in our health care system, and the nurse and the director of hospice felt he would be more comfortable with a male chaplain.

When I drove to the patient's house for my first visit, I found that it was located in the kind of affluent neighborhood in which you would expect a doctor to live. I found the address, and it was a large brick home with a circular drive. An expensive car sat in the driveway, and I pulled in behind it. When I rang the doorbell, it was answered by a man and a very large, long-haired, expensive-looking dog. The good news was that the dog was not aggressive in any way. The bad news was that he freely shed his long, white hair all over my suit. I knew I would have to pull out my trusty lint remover once I left the house.

The man who had greeted me at the door introduced himself as Greg, the patient's husband. The patient, Sylvia, was resting in the master bedroom of the house, being attended to by a nurse's aide. Greg explained that Sylvia was now bedbound, too weak to even sit in a wheelchair. He invited me to follow him into the family room where we could talk without disturbing her. The first thing I noticed was how opulent the home was, with very expensive furniture, valuable-looking artwork on the walls, and what appeared to be artifacts placed prominently in the areas I could see. Even though it was beautifully decorated, the house seemed more like a museum where everything was on display. I felt no warmth in the home.

When I commented on how beautifully the family room was decorated, Greg offered to give me a tour of the house. He proudly pointed out the various decorations and told me where he and Sylvia had bought them while on their trips to different parts of the world. As I listened to Greg, I sensed that he was very proud of his possessions. As you will see later, his love of possessions diminished as time went on.

Another thing that I noticed in the short time I had been with Greg was that he was used to being in control. He had worked hard and trained long to become a doctor. He had that self-confidence that often comes with that kind of accomplishment. He even described himself as being somewhat of a control freak at times. Unfortunately, this would be a real burden for him in the matter of his wife's illness.

We finally sat in the family room and began to discuss Sylvia's condition and the long fight she had waged against her cancer. Greg spoke in clinical terms, like a doctor talking about one of his patients. He explained that she had tried everything she could to beat her cancer, including going out of the country for treatments not approved in the United States. Nothing had stopped that relentless advance of the disease as it continued to ravage her body.

I listened to Greg for a while before asking him about his and his wife's spiritual beliefs. He explained that her spiritual journey was similar to her search for a cure for her cancer. She had researched and delved into various forms of spiritual beliefs, many of which they had encountered on their travels. As far as he knew, she believed in a mixture of the things she had practiced at one time or another. Conversations about spiritual matters were not something they had often shared. As far as his own beliefs, he definitely believed there was a God, but he didn't understand why He would allow this tragedy to happen to them.

Before our visit was over, I asked if I could go into the bedroom and speak to his wife. He was agreeable, but I found that she was sleeping. It would be at a later visit before I would have the opportunity to talk with her.

I visited with Greg and Sylvia at least two times a week because she was very close to death. Greg was having tremendous difficulty dealing with what was happening and what was to come. As my relationship with Greg became more comfortable, I finally decided it was time to have a serious talk about what was really going on in his mind. Thus far, most of his comments had been superficial and vague. When I told him that I sensed anger, and maybe even feelings of guilt, his eyes began to water up and tears ran down his face. It was as if a dam had been breached and the words began to pour out.

Greg was angry with God for allowing his wife's terminal illness at such a young age. They had been enjoying life together so much. She was the soul mate he had searched for over the years, and when he finally found her, their time together had been so brief. I explained to him that his anger was natural and that he should take all his feelings to God. He, above all, understood, and He was big enough to handle it. I didn't have an answer for him as to why God allowed his wife's illness. No matter how badly Greg wanted the answer, he may never receive it in this life. I encouraged him to trust that God is good and has a plan and a purpose for everything He allows in our lives.

Then Greg expressed what had really been torturing him. He said that as a doctor he had saved many lives but now he couldn't save his own wife. This is what hurt him the most, and there was absolutely nothing he could do. In other words, this was something over which he had no control. After he had run out of words to describe what he was feeling, I asked him if I could be perfectly frank with him, and he gave me that freedom.

I encouraged Greg to let go of his guilt for several reasons. First, the truth was that he had never saved anyone's life. Only God could do that. Greg had simply been the instrument God had chosen to use. Second, God is the author of life and of death. He is sovereign and in control, and we are not. His wife's healing, or her death, would be completely up to God. The reality of the situation was that even though he was a doctor, Greg, like any other human being, had to accept God's decision, whatever it may be.

I wasn't sure how Greg had received my words because he was very quiet as tears continued to run down his face. After a few moments, he told me he would have to take some time to process what I had said. He realized I was probably right, but some things were just hard for him to accept. Once again I asked if I could go into the bedroom and pray with his wife, and he gave me permission. One thing that had bothered me during my visits was the fact that Greg never went with me to see his wife, nor had I ever seen him with her. I wasn't sure if this was because it was just too painful for him to see her in her present condition or if it was a fresh reminder that the whole situation was out of his control.

On my last visit with Greg and Sylvia before she died, some things happened that I will never forget. As Greg and I were sitting in the den and talking, he was unusually quiet and pensive. I asked if there was anything he would like to talk about, and almost immediately he waved his arms around and said, "I would trade everything I have here to have my wife back!" And then I held him as he sobbed.

When I went into the bedroom to see Sylvia for the last time, she was drowsy from the pain medication but still able to communicate verbally. I knew it was the last opportunity I would probably have to talk with her about her spiritual condition. I told her that I knew she had examined and practiced many different beliefs, trying to find the answer to spiritual truth, and I wondered if she had found what she had been searching for. With a smile on her face, Sylvia responded, "I found the truth." When I asked what she meant by that, with that smile still on her face, she answered, "I found Jesus. He is the truth." I told her she really had found the truth, and I expressed how happy I was for her. Sylvia was at peace. She closed her eyes, and as I held her hand and prayed for her, I recognized that I would not see her again on this side of heaven. After leaving her room, I felt the joy of knowing her eternity was secure, and I would see her again one day.

I officiated at Sylvia's funeral on a cold, rainy day. As I sat and listened to the harpist playing, I closed my eyes, and I could almost imagine I was in heaven. There was a calmness and a peace in my soul, just knowing that Sylvia was no longer suffering. Her healing had been instant and complete. As for Greg, I spoke with him several times after that, and he was beginning to move forward with his life without Sylvia. During one of our conversations, he expressed his loneliness and wondered if he would ever find anyone like Sylvia again. My answer to him was "No, you won't find anyone like her again, and that shouldn't be your goal. Search for the one God has prepared for you."

I hope he found her.

LIFE LESSON

There are several life lessons we can learn from this story, but to me, the most important one is the understanding that possessions are not important when compared to relationships. Family, friends, and most importantly, our relationship with the Lord are far more valuable than any possession. Having stood at the bedside of many terminally ill people, I have never heard anyone ask to have their possessions brought to where they could see them one more time. On the other hand, I have heard many people ask for a loved one. Jesus spoke of this often in scripture, pointing out the folly of trusting in and holding too tightly to possessions.

For where your treasure is, there your heart will be also. (Matthew 6:21)

REFLECTIONS

CHAPTER 14

In the Strangest Places

Arriving back at my office in the inpatient unit one evening after finishing my scheduled home visits, I checked our census (patient list) to see if there were any new patients. Since there was only one, I decided to go to his room and see if he was awake or if any family members were present. When I knocked on the door, there was no response, so I slowly opened the door and was surprised to find the room was in complete darkness. Using the light from the hall, I walked to the far side of the patient's bed so I could turn on a lamp and check on him. Before I did so, I noticed the shadow of someone sitting on the other side of the bed. The person had not said a word.

I introduced myself, and a woman responded, telling me her name was Myra. She identified herself as the patient's wife. The patient, Arthur, was unresponsive, so I asked her if I could sit and visit with her for a few minutes, and she gave me permission. I pulled a chair up closer, but because the only light in the room was still coming from the hallway, her face remained in the shadows. I began the conversation by asking her some basic information questions. Myra told me that her husband had been ill for a very long time. This had made life extremely difficult for both of them. Even though she would miss him greatly, she felt relief that his suffering would soon be over. As I had heard numerous others testify in the past, she also felt guilty for feeling as she did.

We talked about those feelings for some time. I explained to her that they were normal and that many other people had struggled with them as well. I stressed to her that because she loved Arthur, she wanted what was best for him. Knowing he would never recover from his illness, no longer suffering would be what was best. Her feeling of relief that the end was near was driven by her love for him. After talking for over an hour, I prayed with Myra and Arthur and then left the room, thinking he would probably die overnight and I would not see them again.

To my surprise, Arthur was still lingering the next evening. I went to his room to check on him and to see if Myra was once again at his bedside. I knocked before entering, but as before, I didn't hear a response. I gently pushed the door open and found that the room was in darkness as it had been on the previous evening. Myra was sitting quietly in the shadows next to his bed. She thanked me for coming again.

Our conversation that evening took on a deeper spiritual tone. Myra had not felt God's presence for many years. She now felt that He had abandoned her completely. Arthur was a good man, only in his early sixties, and she couldn't understand how God could let this happen to them when some of the best years of their lives were just beginning. Having heard these same comments from other loved ones to whom I had ministered over the years, I assured Myra that God had not abandoned her. He was present with her and Arthur, every minute of every day. I also assured her that God was aware of her pain and every tear she had shed. She remained silent after I told her this, and I wasn't sure what her silence meant. After we talked a little longer, I prayed with her and Arthur before leaving to visit another patient.

Arthur did die during the night. I didn't see him or Myra again. I wondered if our conversations had any impact on her and if she would even remember them. I could only pray for comfort and peace for her as she dealt with the grief over losing her husband.

A hospice chaplain's schedule is demanding. It is a twenty-four/seven ministry. As a result, we have to put each case behind us and move on the next assignments. I became busy with other cases and soon had to push my conversations with Myra into the back of my mind. One morning as I entered my office and began to look through my mail, I was pleasantly surprised to see that I had received a card from her. She wrote to thank me for being present with her during Arthur's last days. Myra went on to write how grateful she was that I had helped her find her way back to

God. She had found what she had lost as a result of our conversations, sitting in a mostly dark room, at her dying husband's bedside. Upon reading the card, one of the other staff members remarked that God shows up in some of the strangest places.

LIFE LESSON

Yes, God does show up in some of the strangest places, but we should never lose sight of the truth that He is always present, no matter where we are and no matter what the circumstances. As I can testify from my own experiences, we are often so focused on our circumstances or our feelings that we cannot recognize God's presence. We sometimes base His presence in our situation on whether or not we feel it. Sometimes we judge His presence on whether or not we can see Him working. And at other times, we arrive at the conclusion God is not present because we can't hear His voice.

The Bible teaches that God is omniscient (all knowing) and omnipresent (present everywhere at all times). This being the case, we can be assured of His loving presence regardless of our circumstances or our feelings. His presence is not based on feelings but about who He is and the promises He has made.

God doesn't move away from us. We move away from Him. The good news is this promise He has made to each of us: "Never will I leave you; never will I forsake you" (Hebrews 13:5).

You still can't seem to find Him? Then I encourage you to claim this promise found in Jeremiah 29:13. "You will seek me and find me when you seek me with all you heart." And remember God doesn't just show up in the strangest places but in the ordinary places as well.

REFLECTIONS

CHAPTER 15

With a Song on Her Lips

While on call as a chaplain at a large, local hospital, I received a call one night to come to the high-risk pregnancy floor. When I arrived, I encountered a young couple who were still in shock at the loss of their baby who had almost been full term. Both of their parents were present, grieving with them. I prayed for them and offered all the words of comfort I could in such a difficult situation.

As I left their room, I started down the hall toward the chaplain's office. As I passed a room two doors down, I noticed a celebration with laughter, brightly colored balloons, and pictures being taken. A healthy baby had just been born to another young couple. When I saw this and thought of the room I had just left, I couldn't help but think of the contrast: one family was grieving and just a few feet away another family was celebrating. This is the reality of life that happens all around us each day.

As a hospice chaplain, I sometimes saw the same occurrence at our inpatient unit. Some rooms that I entered were occupied by families whose grief was so great that it was palpable. The loss of a loved one was accompanied by tears, sometimes wailing, and an atmosphere I could describe as one of helplessness and hopelessness.

Just down the hall, another family had also lost a loved one, but there was a celebration taking place. The friends and family members were celebrating the homegoing of their loved one. Yes, they would grieve their loss, but they would also feel great joy because they knew that the deceased person was in the presence of the Lord because of his or her faith in the Jesus Christ. They also were confident that they would see their loved one again, this time without ever having to say, "Goodbye" or "See you later."

Such was the case one day when I went to one of our largest rooms at the end of the hall. This large room had been assigned to this patient because she had a very large family who would be visiting each day. Lillian had several children, grandchildren, and even a few great-grandchildren. When you added in all the spouses and friends from her neighborhood and church, you had a crowd.

In fact, when I entered Lillian's room for the first time, I was amazed at the number of people crammed into the room. Not only was the room filled with people, it was filled with music, laughter, and a party atmosphere. Upon my entry, the noise died down for a minute, and I introduced myself as the chaplain. Some of the people present looked like children who had just been caught making too much noise in their bedroom when they should have been sleeping. I tried to lighten the atmosphere by telling them that my feelings were hurt because there was a party going on and I hadn't been invited. I was soon surrounded by people who welcomed me and made me feel like a part of the family. I eventually made my way to Lillian's bed, where I spent a few minutes talking with her.

I enjoyed visiting with Lillian and her family the next few days. There was always a lot of laughter, joking, and joy. Lillian always had a smile on her face and a kind word. She seemed to be in perfect peace with the fact that she would soon be leaving this life. She was prepared, and her family was prepared. They knew there would be a welcoming committee and a celebration when Lillian got to heaven. The family was also planning on having a party for her here.

Their peace and joy came from a deep, abiding faith in the Lord. Instead of seeing death as something to be feared, they saw it as something to be celebrated. For me, visiting with them was like arriving at a refreshing oasis. At the end of each visit, I would gather everyone in a circle, and holding hands, I would lead in prayer. Inevitably someone else would also pray, and at times I felt as if an old-time revival had broken out.

Lillian and her family told me how much she loved singing the old hymns. She would walk around her house singing them most of the day, and the family members never grew tired of hearing her. They often sang along with her. They continued to sing them with her when she arrived at hospice. It was such a sweet sound to hear.

One evening, as I entered her room to check on her and her family, the same party atmosphere was present. I noticed though that this time it was accompanied with tears, which I soon learned were tears of joy. Lillian had made it safely home. She had taken a very gentle breath, almost a sigh, with a smile on her face. The angels had escorted her into the presence of the Lord she had loved and served so faithfully for so many years.

But this wasn't the end of the story. Lillian had been unresponsive for a couple of days, but just before she took her final breath, she very softly, almost in a whisper, began to sing "Amazing Grace." The family had been in awe of what they were hearing. Faith gave them the assurance that Lillian was now experiencing the fullness of God's amazing grace. They were all so thankful that she left this life with a song on her lips, a song they felt sure she was singing to Jesus Himself.

LIFE LESSON

It has been my experience that people grieve in many different ways. Much of how they do this has to do with their faith and their beliefs about life and death. There is no right or wrong way to grieve, unless it leads a person to be harmful to themselves or others or it becomes an obsession that cannot be overcome. In such cases, the grieving person should seek professional counsel immediately.

God gave us the ability to grieve. Grief is the result of losing someone or something we love. Grief is part of the healing process after suffering loss. In the book of Ecclesiastes, Solomon wrote that there is "a time to weep and a time to laugh, a time to mourn and a time to dance" (Ecclesiastes 3:4). Grief, while never gone completely, must never stop us from moving on with a productive and joyful life. It is what our deceased loved one would want for us and what God would want for us.

All of us have, or will, one day suffer the loss of a loved one. It's part of the human experience and a natural part of the life/death cycle. In my own life, when I have lost loved ones to death, one of God's promises I have claimed is Psalm 30:5. "Weeping may remain for a night, but rejoicing comes in the morning." This verse has brought me much peace and comfort over the years. May it do the same for you.

REFLECTIONS

CHAPTER 16

A Hero's Homegoing

I received the call from one of our hospice social workers the Friday afternoon of the weekend before Thanksgiving. It was a very busy time, and I had a large caseload of home patients, along with a sudden surge in new admissions in my territory. With the holidays coming, I knew I would be pushed to see all my assigned patients and get all the charting done within the required time. The last thing I needed at that time was an urgent call from a social worker asking that I see another new patient as soon as possible. I consider what I did as a hospice chaplain to be a very great privilege and a blessing afforded to me by God, but surely He knew my schedule!

But sure enough, the social worker explained that she had a new male patient who wanted to see a chaplain as quickly as possible. When she told me where the patient lived, I breathed a sigh of relief because his home was outside of my assigned territory. My relief didn't last very long though because she explained that he wanted a male chaplain, and I was the only one on staff at that time. I took all the information and assured her I would call the patient before making my next visit. I was feeling a little overwhelmed at this point, so I did what I always did when I felt this way. I found a parking lot to pull into, and as I sat in my car, I prayed. As usually happened, a sense of peace and calmness came over me as God, through His Spirit, assured me that He did know my schedule. Imagine that! *But God* (there's my favorite phrase again) wasn't through. He also assured me that He knew where I needed to be and who I needed to see. I knew from experience that if I was led by

His Spirit rather than my own agenda, everything would work out as it should.

My Heavenly Father knows best, so feeling humbled and a little chastised, I used my cell phone to call the new patient's home. His wife answered and thanked me for calling and explained that her husband was very anxious to talk with a chaplain. She wanted to know if I could come that afternoon. Obviously, this wasn't what I wanted to hear, but I also heard a sense of urgency in her voice that led me to set a time later that afternoon to visit with them.

When I arrived at the patient's home and rang the doorbell, I was met by the patient's wife, Evelyn, who invited me in. She was very gracious, thanking me for coming so soon, and she made me feel comfortable and welcome. After telling me about some of the beautiful Christmas decorations that already adorned their home, she took me into the sitting area to meet her husband.

Ben was sitting on a couch, and just like his wife, he thanked me for coming so quickly. He invited me to sit down across from him so we could talk. It wasn't long before I felt as if I had known this couple all my life. They were so humble and down to earth and had so many entertaining stories to share about their lives. They had at one time owned a dairy farm, but eventually it became too much for them to keep and they regretfully had to sell it. Now they were retired, but because of his failing health, they were pretty much confined to home. They enjoyed being together, and the love they shared was so obvious. They also enjoyed spending time with their daughter, son, and grandchildren when possible.

After some extremely enjoyable conversation, I sat forward in the chair and asked Ben why he had called for me. He began by explaining that he had been diagnosed with cancer, and he and his family knew he only had a short time to live—a few months at most. He then began to tell me about his doubts concerning death and the hereafter and why he had those doubts. The patient had been a pilot during WWII and was a recipient of the Distinguished Flying Cross. Ben had faced death many times during his service. He had seen many of his friends die as their planes were shot down in combat. He knew the reality of death and was accepting of that. He also knew many of these men were probably not Christians, but they were good men who had given their lives for their country. In addition, having the opportunity to travel in many parts of the world, he had met men and women who were members of faiths other than Christianity. He had known Muslims, Jews, Hindus, and people of other faiths or no faith at all. They were good, moral people who had lived good lives and done good things to help others.

As a result of this, he could not accept the belief that these good people were going, or had gone, to hell because they did not believe in Jesus Christ. The Bible's claim that faith in Jesus is the only way to heaven was not something he could easily accept. Why would God send good people to hell? Why were there no other routes to heaven? Surely God made allowance for the good things people did on earth. He was about to die, and he was seeking answers. As he told me, "I want to make sure I get it right before I die, because then it will be too late. I wanted to see a chaplain because I need answers. If you have any, I would like to hear them."

It was then I knew God had arranged another divine appointment for me. It was also then that I began to pray and ask God, through His Holy Spirit, to give me the words I needed to share with Ben. Here was a true American hero, a man's man, and war had not frightened him as much as not finding the right answer before he stepped into eternity. I couldn't help but think what a difficult thing it must be for such a man to humble himself before another man and acknowledge his fear and his lack of answers. I was humbled to think God had given me this opportunity.

I very quietly and gently began to share with Ben what the Bible had to say about salvation through faith in Jesus Christ, sharing scriptures and examples from my own experience. He listened intently without interruption, his eyes focused on mine. I soon noticed Ben was tiring, and I knew I had given him a lot to absorb. Remembering that he had a very analytical mind, I decided to leave him with some things to consider. I first reiterated that Jesus had made a very bold claim when He said, "I am the way and the truth and the life. No one comes to the Father except through me" (John 14:6). So as the great apologist C. S. Lewis had alluded to, each person, upon hearing Jesus's claim, must decide if Jesus was a liar, a lunatic, or Lord as He claimed to be. Did Jesus know He wasn't the Son of God and His claim was false? Did He just set out to pull off the greatest hoax ever known to man? Was He a lunatic who truly thought He was the Son of God when, in truth, He wasn't? Or is Jesus truly the Son of God just as He claimed to be, and His bold claim is truth? I left one other thought with him. If there were ways to get to heaven other than faith in Jesus Christ, such as good works or being a good person, why then did Jesus have to come to earth and suffer such a horrible death on the cross?

I felt the Holy Spirit telling me to leave these things with Ben to consider. The rest would be up to him. Over the next few days, I prayed diligently for Ben, asking God's Spirit to reveal truth to him and for him to respond to the truth with faith. Two days after Thanksgiving, I received a call from Ben's nurse, who said he wanted to talk with me once again as soon as possible. I adjusted my schedule so I could see him that afternoon. I didn't know what to expect, but I was hoping for some good news.

When I arrived at his home, his wife once more escorted me into the room where Ben was sitting. He thanked me again for coming on such short notice, and since he wasn't one to waste time, he immediately began to tell me why he had asked me to return. He had not called earlier because he didn't want to interrupt my Thanksgiving, but since our talk, he had been considering all the things I had shared with him. After much consideration and weighing all the options, the things I had told him began to make sense. He had finally reached the decision that Jesus's claim to be the Son of God and the only path to heaven was true. Once he had reached this decision, he felt a new peace, but he still didn't know what he needed to do to receive eternal life. With his life slowly dwindling away, he wanted to make sure he was ready when it ended.

I told Ben how glad I was about his decision and then led him in prayer as he confessed he was a sinner. He acknowledged Jesus as the only way to heaven and asked Jesus to forgive him of his sins and give him eternal life. When he had finished, I prayed, thanking God for Ben's salvation and for the peace and joy that could now be his. When I looked at Ben, I saw the smile on his face and the tears on the face of his wife who had been praying for him for many years. She was so excited. What a great Christmas present!

Ben then thanked me for sharing with him without pushing, and he stated that God knew exactly who to send to talk with him. I made sure he knew that God received all the praise and glory for bringing us together and for his salvation. It was a "God thing" all the way. Coincidence that we came together? I don't think so. Just another divine appointment.

Ben went to be with the Lord a few weeks later, and I was honored to officiate at his memorial service and then his interment at the National Cemetery. Each time I think of Ben, I am reminded of what an awesome God we serve. I am also excited I will be seeing Ben again one day on the other side. Then I'll have all eternity to hear the rest of the stories about his adventures as a pilot.

LIFE LESSON

As I stated earlier, Ben was a true American hero, but as great as his accomplishments had been, he still needed salvation through Jesus Christ. In Acts 10:34, we read, "Then Peter began to speak: "I now realize how true it is that God does not show favoritism." We all come before him on level ground, regardless of our economic status, education, musical or athletic ability, or any other earthly standard by which people tend to judge other people. No matter how great our accomplishments on earth, they won't matter in eternity if we enter it without Jesus. But on the other hand, the good news is that no matter where we have been or what we have done, God still offers forgiveness and salvation to anyone who will confess, repent, and place his or her faith in His Son, Jesus Christ. You don't have to be a hero.

REFLECTIONS

CHAPTER 17

With His Boots On

Seth was only in his thirties when he was admitted to the inpatient unit. He had been diagnosed with inoperable brain cancer. The rapidly progressing disease was already taking its toll on his cognitive functions when I first met him. At times he was agitated and confused, but these times were interspersed with times of lucidity which is often the case in these situations. During one of my visits with Seth, I found him to be a very shy person. At first it was difficult to get him to open up and share his thoughts and feelings.

One morning, as I stopped by to check on him and pray with him, it was as if I was talking with a different person. Maybe I had earned his trust with my previous visits. Maybe he recognized his time was short and wanted to say the things he felt were important while he could still verbalize them. Whatever brought about the change, I was pleasantly surprised and grateful for the opportunity to listen.

Seth spoke of having often taken the wrong path during his younger years, a path that led to a battle with alcohol and drugs. He expressed his regret over these bad decisions and the hurt his actions had caused his family and others who had tried to help him over the years. When he was diagnosed with a terminal illness, it was a stunning blow. At first he felt it was God's way of punishing him for the bad things he had done. Even though he also felt anger over his life being cut short, he believed he deserved what had happened.

Seth had been married, but his addictions destroyed his relationship with his wife, and they were soon divorced. He had a young son who he saw occasionally. Even though he greatly loved his son, he knew he was a poor role model for him. Seth just never knew how to express his love in the appropriate ways. In conclusion, Seth was approaching the end of his life with many regrets and shameful memories.

During one of my previous visits with Seth, I had met his sister, Dawn. I was able to observe her dedication to Seth's care, coming each day to spend time with him and to ensure his needs were being met. I had the opportunity to talk with her one day outside of Seth's presence. She confirmed all that he had told me. She also spoke of Seth's gentle spirit and his willingness to help others when he wasn't under the influence of the "demon on his back." He was the big brother who had always protected her when they were growing up. Despite all he had done, she still had happy memories of their childhood and high school years. She would always love him and was committed to being with him until the end.

Seth continued to decline, and I recognized that his days of being able to communicate were rapidly coming to an end. Feeling that I had built a good enough rapport with him by this time, I decided to try to talk with him about his spiritual beliefs. At first Seth seemed reluctant to talk about this topic, and I just sat silently with him, allowing him the time to process his thoughts. I could tell he was struggling with what to say, if anything at all. Finally, with tears running down his face, he told me he had gone to church with his mother as a child. He had even made a profession of faith and been baptized. Then he acknowledged he had not lived like a Christian. He had recently had a lot of time to think about what would happen to him when he died, and he had decided God could not forgive him for all the bad things he had done. He felt he had wasted the life God had given him.

As I listened to Seth, I couldn't help but think of how many times I had sat at the bedside of dying people and heard the same feelings expressed. They are often said with a feeling of hopelessness and fear. Sometimes they are spoken with a sense of desperation, seeking some small glimmer of hope. As always, I was so thankful I had good news to share with each one of these hurting people. The good news was always that God loves them, and He is willing and even eager to forgive them and offer them eternal life if they will only ask. It is never too late, until a person takes his or her final breath. Fortunately, some have listened and taken advantage of God's invitation, but sadly others have refused. Seth eagerly and gratefully accepted. The very next day, he became comatose, but some of the last words he had spoken were life changing for him. He asked God to forgive him of his sins and give him eternal life.

In my visits with Seth, I had noticed a cowboy hat lying on the bed. I had asked about this and learned that Seth loved country and western music. His wardrobe consisted of blue jeans, cowboy shirts, and boots. He jokingly said he had been a cowboy living in the Wild West during his previous life. So this is why I wasn't surprised when, on the morning when Seth died, his sister asked if she could dress him in his cowboy attire. She also asked if I would perform a small memorial service at his bedside. I was honored to do so, and when I entered the room, sure enough, there lay Seth wearing his jeans and cowboy shirt with his cowboy hat on his chest. And yes, he had on his boots.

Seth's sister, mother, and son were among the small gathering in his room. We had a very sweet and intimate home going celebration for him, with tears, laughter, and good memories. As I looked at Seth, I was so grateful he had made things right with God. I pictured him riding his horse into the sunset.

LIFE LESSON

Most every one of us will come to the end of our lives with some regrets. This is just a part of the human condition. However, these regrets do not have to identify who we are or how we will end our days on earth. When counseling with people, I always encourage them, if necessary, to go to the people they feel they have hurt or failed in some way, acknowledge what they have done, and ask forgiveness. Try to make things right while there is still time. Sometimes people are accepting and will respond with forgiveness. Others may respond negatively. However, if we have done the best we can do to make things right, there is nothing more we can do. The really good news is that God never turns down a sincere heart who seeks forgiveness. If our relationship with Him is right, we can approach life now, and at its end, with confidence and peace without regret.

> If we confess our sins, he is faithful and just and will forgive us our sins and purify us from all unrighteousness. (1 John 1:9)

REFLECTIONS

CHAPTER 18

The Strength of True Love

Bill had been one of my home patients for several months. He was very difficult to catch up with in order to schedule a visit. Bill was an active man. The terminal cancer with which he had been diagnosed hadn't seemed to slow him down one bit. He spent much of his time working in his yard, cutting grass, pruning shrubs, and doing anything else that needed to be done.

Once I was able to pin him down and visit with him, the time was always enjoyable, but often challenging. Why challenging? Bill was a self-taught Bible scholar, and he loved to discuss and debate scripture. Even though I was seminary-trained pastor, I found Bill to be a very tough debater, and he kept me on my toes. What I appreciated most about our debates was the fact that we could disagree agreeably and still love one another as brothers in Christ. We always ended the visits in good spirits, even though there were times when I returned to my car feeling like I had been back in seminary.

I met Bill's wife, Sally, only once at their home before he had to be admitted to the inpatient unit. Sally was also very active and enjoyed traveling and shopping with her friends and relatives. That one encounter though made it clear that she and Bill were still very much in love, after more than fifty years of marriage. It was also clear they both had the same love for God and His Word. They were an inspiration to me and I'm sure to just about anyone who met them. I once told Bill I wanted to be just like him when I grew up.

Bill's cancer finally weakened him to the point he could no longer take care of himself. Sally, who also had health issues of her own, was unable to provide for all his needs. Much to their distress, Bill was admitted to the inpatient facility. Unfortunately, Sally's condition quickly worsened, and she had to be admitted to the hospital located next to the hospice facility. This loving couple, who had been so close for so many years, was now separated by two blocks. For them, it must have seemed like thousands of miles, an impossible barrier to overcome.

But true love provides a strength that can overcome what appear to be impossible barriers. We often think of this being true for young lovers, but my experience has taught me that it is just as true, if not more so, for those who have been in love for a lifetime. As weak and close to death as Bill was, he wanted nothing more than to see his beautiful bride one more time. The hospice staff would always try to meet any reasonable requests when possible, but their first priority was always the safety and comfort of the patient. Bill was so emotional and adamant in his request that the staff soon decided that, with the assistance of his two daughters, Bill could make the short but difficult trip to his wife's hospital room.

The hospital was only two blocks from the hospice facility but it was uphill all the way. So the staff moved Bill into a wheelchair and made sure he was covered well so he would not get cold, and off they went. His devoted daughters pushed Bill in his wheelchair up the hill, which was no easy trip for either them or Bill. Even though they were all exhausted by the time they arrived at Sally's room in the hospital, it was soon evident the reunion was worth the effort.

Bill, in his wheelchair, sat at Sally's side. Even though they were both very sick and very weak, there was no doubt of the love and devotion they shared for one another as they looked into each other's eyes. Bill was too weak for much conversation, but after a few minutes of silence that spoke greater than words, he reached out his hand and took Sally's hand. Finally, when it was apparent Bill was becoming weary and needed to return to his bed at the hospice facility, he asked his daughters to help him stand. He then leaned over the bed and gave a final kiss to the love of his life. Both Bill and Sally knew this was the last kiss they would share this side of heaven, but they also had the peace of knowing one day they would see each other again.

Bill's daughters returned him to the hospice unit where he died a couple of days later. Shortly thereafter, Sally was admitted to the hospice inpatient unit, where I had the blessing of meeting with her and her daughters. They shared with me how Bill and Sally had met as "youngsters." Upon hearing all that had transpired, I told them it was a true, modern-day love story. Sally went home to be with Jesus shortly thereafter. She was with Bill once again. I couldn't help but smile as I thought of their first kiss in heaven.

LIFE LESSON

We often think of the passion and joy of young love, and it certainly should never be scoffed at or minimized. But neither should we scoff at or minimize "old love," the love that has aged through the years like a fine wine. Old love has had the opportunity of experiencing great times of joy to be shared with grateful hearts. But I think even more important are the times of difficulty old love has shared, those times when love is truly tested. It is during these times when we find out if the love expressed and the commitment made when young are the real things. There is a beauty and a dignity in old love that touches the heart and stirs the emotions in a very special way words cannot adequately express. Ask me. I know.

May your fountain be blessed, and may you rejoice in the wife of your youth. (Proverbs 5:18)

REFLECTIONS

CHAPTER 19

Unexplainable Things

Over the years, I have encountered many unexplainable events, especially in the spiritual sphere. My experiences as a hospice chaplain have affirmed to me there is an afterlife, that death is not the end. The body dies, but the spirit lives on in another realm. It is this knowledge that gives us hope, the assurance that this life is not all there is but something comes afterward that is beyond our comprehension and imagination.

The spiritual sometimes becomes a part of the physical in unexpected ways, as was the case when Beverly's husband, Jack, died at the inpatient unit. I had visited with Beverly as she stood at the bedside of her comatose husband. Brain cancer had taken its toll and was soon to destroy and bring to an end the very life on which it had thrived. Like so many in these situations, Beverly was torn between wanting her husband to get better and live and the hope he would soon die and be released from his suffering. But there was much more to her story.

In my visits with Beverly and Jack, she was always extremely nervous and often tearful, which was understandable under the circumstances, but she had the appearance of a trapped animal. Her head was always cast downward, and her eyes darted around, from place to place, as if she expected something or someone to attack her. Finally, one day as I was talking with her in the hallway outside of Jack's room, the floodgates opened, and her story began to pour out.

Jack was not Beverly's first husband. She had been divorced years before and had really not intended to marry again, but Jack had been so nice, treating her in a way she had never been treated before. He showed her respect, as if she was special. That is, until after they were married. It was almost as if someone had flipped a switch and Jack became someone else. He took total control of their finances, only allowing her to have money as needed for groceries and other necessities. Jack would fly into a rage at the smallest things and became verbally abusive at first, but this soon led to physical abuse. Beverly couldn't believe what had happened and didn't know what to do about it. She felt hopelessly trapped, as many women do in this type of relationship.

It took all the courage she could muster, but she finally made the decision to leave Jack, even though she was afraid of what he would do once he discovered her intentions. But fate intervened, and Beverly was once again placed in what appeared to her to be an impossible situation. Jack was diagnosed with terminal cancer. What could she do? What would people think if she left her husband just when he found out he was dying? Even though Jack had treated her badly, how could she leave him now in his greatest time of need? Guilt became her constant companion. She wanted to flee and get away from it all, but she knew she couldn't.

Beverly didn't have a clue what the future would hold for her and Jack. As his disease progressed, he became less able to care for himself. She had to do things for him she never thought she could do. His anger became even more extreme, and even though he was now too weak to be physically abusive, his verbal abuse rose to a new level. She couldn't do anything right, and she began to feel as if the nightmare would never end. Much later, after having the time to process all that had happened since she married Jack, Beverly wondered if his sudden change in behavior had been related to his sickness long before he was diagnosed. The possibility that he may not have been purposely hurting her helped Beverly find some comfort in all she had endured.

By the time Jack was admitted to the inpatient unit, Beverly was physically exhausted and at the end of her emotional rope. She found herself in what she would describe, in veiled terms, as a love-hate relationship with her husband. The emotional confusion she was experiencing was leading her toward a complete emotional breakdown.

As Beverly told me her story, tears ran down her face, and she eventually began to sob so hard she could not continue. I held her in my arms as her tears soaked my suit coat, and I softly spoke words of comfort, assuring her she had done more than could ever have been expected of her. Beverly's daughter had been sitting in the room next to Jack's bed. She stepped into the hall and said she thought he was gone. I left Beverly in the hall, entered his room, and found that Jack had taken his last breath. I called the nurse to come pronounce him. During all this, Beverly declined returning to the room.

A few minutes later, when I stepped back into the hall to talk with Beverly about arrangements, she was wide-eyed and white as a ghost. I feared she was about to faint, and I tried to take her arm and help her to a chair, but she seemed to be frozen into place. Then, lifting her arm, she pointed down the hall and said, "I just saw him. He just walked down the hall with another man, and they went around the corner." I asked, "You just saw who?" Beverly responded, "My husband. He was just walking down the hall talking with another man, and they went around the corner." I said, "Beverly, your husband just died and his body is still in the bed in his room." Beverly looked at me and with a face that left no room for doubt and yelled out, "I know my husband, and I know his walk and what the back of his head looks like! That was him walking down the hall!" All I could say was, "Beverly, I believe you."

I stayed with Beverly and her daughter until the funeral home removed Jack's body. I didn't see her again until several months later. I had just returned to the inpatient unit after visiting several home patients. As I started toward my office, I looked down the hall toward the nurse's station, and I saw her almost at the same time she saw me. We walked toward each other and met in the hall just down from the nurse's station. When I asked why she was at the inpatient unit, she explained she had come to visit a friend who had just been admitted. She then began to cry, and I told her how sorry I was. I didn't know if she was crying for her friend or if revisiting the inpatient facility had brought back some painful memories. Beverly suddenly hugged me and told me she was crying because I had believed her. When I asked what she meant, Beverly said, "You were the only one who believed me when I said I had seen my husband walking down the hall. I just wanted to thank you for that."

LIFE LESSON

Did Beverly see her husband walking down the hall with another man right after he had died? I still believe she did. But who was the other man? Do people really see angels who have come to escort them to their heavenly home? Do they really hear the beautiful music of heaven just before dying? Did we really feel the soft breeze hit our faces just at the moment a person's soul departed from its no longer living body? Some things are just unexplainable.

> Then Jesus told him, "Because you have seen me, you have believed; blessed are those who have not seen and yet have believed." (John 20:29)

REFLECTIONS

CHAPTER 20

A Promise Kept

They had been married when they were teenagers, and as often happens in these kinds of marriages, everyone said it wouldn't last. They were too young and didn't understand how difficult married life could be. Besides, they had no money, and as everyone knows, you can't live on love alone. But they had proved all the naysayers wrong. They had stayed together through the good times and the bad and had raised their family. Now it was time for them to enjoy the fruits of their labor. Unfortunately, life has a way of throwing us some pretty nasty curveballs, and that is what happened to Ken and Christy.

Everything had been going well for a time, with lots of family get-togethers, the sharing of love, and laughter, and the future looked bright. But Ken had not been feeling well. He didn't have the stamina he usually had, and he had begun to have headaches, something that had never been an issue with him before. He finally decided to go have a checkup, and that was when the unthinkable occurred. Ken was diagnosed with brain cancer.

He had always been a very upbeat and competitive guy, and he quickly decided he would not let this disease win the battle. He would fight it with every tool available to him. He promised his sweet wife that they would win in the end. They also had their very strong faith and a supportive faith community to help them in this battle of life and death. But after surgery, and using all the tools available to them, the doctors had to give Ken and his family the grim news. There was nothing else that could be done. They recommended hospice so he could be kept as comfortable as possible.

That is how I came to meet this remarkable family. When I first visited with Ken, he was restless and not responsive to my presence. I stood at his bedside, holding his hand, and told him God loved him. While I was there, I offered a prayer for both him and his family. I made a mental note to try to stop back by his room later that evening to see if I could meet his family. I had no idea what a special treat meeting them would be and what an incredible journey I was about to take with them.

I didn't get back to his room that evening as I had hoped, but I did make it there later the next morning. Ken was resting peacefully, and the morning sun was shining through the glass door of his room. There were several people already present. They were laughing, talking, and just enjoying being together. I jokingly remarked that someone was obviously having a party. They welcomed me in, and before I knew it, I felt like part of the family. Their joy and enthusiasm were contagious. I began to look forward to every opportunity to spend time with them. You couldn't be around them without being uplifted and encouraged. It was like mainlining a shot of joy.

During my visits with them, Christy and their children told many stories of the good times they had shared together. These were times of laughter mixed with tears. They had a lot of good memories, and they even told some stories on Ken. I am sure he would love to have been able to respond to them with a little embellishment of his own. They were close-knit and supportive of one another. They also kept expressing their gratitude for everyone who was caring for Ken. They demonstrated this through their heartfelt words of appreciation to the staff who had very difficult jobs and who often felt unappreciated. Ken's room soon became like an oasis, a place of refreshment, like a clear stream of cold water in a hot, dry desert.

One evening as I was visiting with his family, Christy reminisced about her and Ken's marriage as teens. They had always promised they would one day get married again, a renewal of their vows. Somehow the time had flown by, and they had been so busy with life and raising their kids, it had never happened. She had always told him she would be just as eager to marry him again as she had been the first time. She regretted that their renewal of vows would never happen. As I listened to the sadness in her voice and saw the faraway look in her eyes, my own heart was touched with empathy.

Suddenly I realized I had to do something, and without hesitation I said, "Christy, we can do a renewal of vows right here, right now. You and Ken can keep your promise to each other." She looked at me as if I had lost my mind, and she asked, "Really? How?" I told her I would go to my office and get my Bible, and when I came back we would have a ceremony right next to the bed. What better time could there be since her children were present and the room was filled with other family members and friends? I could see the excitement in her eyes as she said, "Let's do it!"

As I walked to my office, I began asking myself what I had just done. How could we have a ceremony when Ken was unable to respond? I knew he would be able to hear us, but he wouldn't even be able to say, "I do." It was too late to turn back, so I just decided to wing it, trusting God would give me an idea and the words to say once we got started.

When I returned to Ken's room with my Bible, there was a festive atmosphere in the room. Everyone was excited and immediately began gathering around the bed. Christy reached out and took Ken's hand in her own as we began. When it came time for Ken to respond to the vows I had just shared, I looked down at him and said, "Ken, I accept your silence and the smile on your face as affirmation that you agree with everything I have said." With a beautiful smile on her face and tears in her eyes, Christy also affirmed her vows. I then pronounced them "still husband and wife" and told Christy she could now kiss her groom, which she did. Those gathered to witness the ceremony broke out in cheers and clapping. There were tears and hugs for all.

As I was returning to my office after the celebration, I thought it would be nice if Christy had something to remind her of the day she and Ken had kept their promise and renewed their vows. So I picked up one of the beautiful prayer shawls some of our volunteers had knitted to give to our families. I went back to their room and presented it to Christy as a gift to memorialize that very special day.

Ken went to be with the Lord a few days later, and while there were tears, the family rejoiced at his homegoing. Their faith had brought them this far, and it would continue to provide them with the comfort and peace they would need in the days ahead. Christy and her family once again expressed their gratitude for the compassion and care given by the hospice staff. What they didn't realize is that they had given much more to us than we could ever have given to them. We, as staff, also rejoiced in Ken's homegoing, but we all knew we would sorely miss his family and the way they had blessed each one of us.

LIFE LESSON

People are often brought into our lives for a season and for a purpose, and then they are gone. We had our season with this wonderful family, and it was one we will all remember with warmth and affection. The privilege of performing a renewal of Ken and Christy's marriage vows will always be one of my favorite memories as well. They had made a promise to each other, and that promise was kept. I have to wonder how many of us have made promises that have never been fulfilled. Maybe that promise was part of a marriage vow but it has not been kept as it should. Why not start today, before it is too late?

> When a man makes a vow to the Lord or takes an oath to obligate himself by a pledge, he must not break his word but must do everything he said. (Numbers 30:2)

REFLECTIONS

CHAPTER 21

Angels Come in All Sizes

When I first reached my new home patient by phone, I was totally caught off guard. I had read the admission notes and knew the patient was a female in her seventies who had been diagnosed with terminal cancer. I had anticipated a family member would answer the phone, but even if the patient answered, I had expected her to at least sound weak. What I got instead was a jolt of energy coming through the phone! When I asked to speak to Amelia, she told me it was her speaking, and she reeled off her full name with a very pronounced accent that also caught me by surprise. In fact, she talked so fast that this, combined with her accent, made it difficult for me to understand her at first. I later learned she was originally from the Philippines.

Trying to regain my composure, I told her who I was and explained that I was calling to see if I could make an appointment to come visit with her. She laughed loudly and said I was welcome to come see her if I could catch up with her, because she was a very busy lady. She then began outlining all the activities in which she was involved, most of which revolved around her different ministries in her Catholic church. As I listened, I kept thinking that this really couldn't be the patient. I was sure someone was playing a joke on me.

When she finally slowed down and I was able to get a word in, I secured a date and time for my first visit. Amelia made it very clear, however, that she was a faithful Catholic and her priest took good care of her. She wasn't interested in anyone trying to convert her or preach to her. I assured her that, as chaplains, we were nondenominational and only came to offer any additional spiritual support we could. When the conversation was finished, at the time of her choosing, I was completely exhausted!

Amelia lived in an apartment built for her in her daughter's basement. As I approached their home, I did so with some anxiety. After her warnings to me about her faith, I knew this visit was only a test. She would listen and observe and decide whether or not she wanted me to come back. I was intimidated, and I hadn't even met her. When she greeted me at the door of her apartment, I was surprised once again. She was tiny! How could that much energy possibly be contained in someone so small? She invited me in, told me where to sit, and began talking about her activities with her church. She would rise early each morning and go to the church to make sure everything was ready for the mass. She also helped train new people to do the tasks and had appointed herself supervisor over them to assure everything was done just the way the priest liked for them to be done. Amelia expressed her observation that most of the young people were not dependable, either coming late to prepare or not preparing properly. In other words, she let me know under no uncertain terms that no one else could perform the job as well as she could. Interspersed in her conversation was praise for her Lord and Savior, Jesus Christ. You couldn't be with her for more than a minute without knowing she was a woman of deep faith.

In addition, Amelia was very involved in visiting the shut-ins of the church and those who were sick. She did not consider herself to fit into either of those categories. She baked for them and did whatever she could to make sure they knew they were loved and not forgotten. She was every preacher's (or priest's) dream member. Amelia was like the Energizer bunny.

My primary ministry on that first visit was to provide a listening ear, but finally she began to quiz me on my background and what I had to offer as a chaplain. As the visit was finally coming to an end, a time decided by Amelia, who appeared to be in control of most every situation, I asked if she would allow me to pray for her. I could tell she struggled with whether or not to allow this since I wasn't a priest, but she finally agreed. I felt as if I had overcome a major hurdle in our relationship. I must have passed her test, because when I asked if I could come visit with her again, she gave permission.

Over the next few months, our relationship grew, and we were able to openly talk like old friends. In fact, if I didn't visit when Amelia thought it was time, she would tell her nurse to call and remind me. Before long, Amelia began to share some of her deepest feelings. She never lost hope that God would heal her, but she was also accepting of her fate if He decided to wait until she went to heaven. She was determined to stay active, particularly in her church, for as long as she could. Amelia was one of the most determined people I have ever known, and her love for the Lord and His church was without bounds. As I watched her decline, I recognized that it was this love that kept her going.

We soon settled into a ritual that was, naturally, of her making. It started on the next visit when I arrived to find she had prepared a meal for me. It was a delicious offering of her native country's cuisine. I had already had lunch and wasn't the least bit hungry, but she had been so gracious to prepare it that I had no choice but to accept. After piling my plate with food and giving me a glass of a wonderful fruit drink that was also common to her country, Amelia told me where to sit, and she sat across from me. I waited for a minute before offering a prayer of thanksgiving, thinking Amelia would prepare a plate for herself. When she just sat there looking at me, I asked if she was going to join me. Amelia answered that she wasn't hungry. She had prepared the meal for her chaplain. I was deeply honored.

Even though I told her more than once that a meal was not necessary, she would prepare one and have it ready by the time I arrived for each visit. She would then sit and watch me enjoy it, and enjoy it I did! Every one of them was a delight to my taste buds. I learned quickly to go with an empty stomach, because one helping would never be enough. Amelia would always make sure I had a second helping. I could tell she found great joy each time I stuffed myself. I always gave her praise for being such a wonderful cook.

As Amelia's strength began to wane, I continued to ask her to stop preparing the meals before my visit. I knew how hard it had to be for her, but she persisted until the time came when she was just too weak to cook. The day I arrived and she apologized for not having something prepared for me to eat, I knew she was on the final leg of her journey home. I could tell by her face that she knew this as well.

It was during this time that she also began to share some of her life story with me. She was born in the Philippines, and as a child during the occupation of the Japanese in WWII, she and her family lived in fear of their lives. She saw many atrocities carried out by their occupiers. She related the day her family watched as her uncle was executed, and they had fully expected to be next. Amelia's life had not been easy. It was her faith and her tenacity that had brought her through. While she had a gentle and loving spirit, she was also tough as nails. She was a survivor, and she fought her illness with that same determination, but this was the one battle she would not win. Amelia knew though that even if the cancer ended her life here on earth, she would still win in the end, because she would be with the Lord Jesus Christ, the One she loved and had served so faithfully.

Amelia eventually became bedbound and was under heavy sedation for pain. Her wish was to die at home, and her daughter was committed to seeing that her wish was honored. On the day of my last visit with her, Amelia was alert but lethargic. I stood at her bedside, holding her hand. We talked about heaven and what it would be like. Amelia couldn't wait to see Jesus face-to-face. She had no fear. She knew the end of her life on earth was very near, but she was at perfect peace, trusting the God who had been so faithful her entire life.

I could see she was tiring, so I assured her that if I didn't see her again on this side, I would see her on the other. She smiled and shook her head in agreement, and then she told me she had something for me. She told me to hold out my hand, and she placed a bronze-looking coin in it. I looked at it and saw that it had an angel imprinted on both sides. She told me it was a reminder that my angel would always be looking after me, and so would she. I thanked her and told her I would always treasure it and keep it with me as a reminder, not only of the angels but also of the love and friendship we had shared. I then offered prayer, thanking God for bringing her into my life and asking that He give her a safe journey home. When I had finished praying, I looked into her eyes one more time and told her I loved her. She told me the same. I could see peace there and the anticipation of going to her real home in heaven. I never saw Amelia again in this life, but I find comfort in knowing I will see her again one day. As for the coin, I have carried it with me every day since she gave it to me. Every time I look at it, I am reminded of our times together, and a smile comes to my face. I have often wondered if she was my angel, the one who would always be looking after me. Then I feel the comfort of her presence. After all, angels come in all sizes.

LIFE LESSON

Yes, I believe in angels because the Bible tells us they exist. I also believe that each of us has a guardian angel watching over us twenty-four/seven. Was Amelia my guardian angel or just a small bundle of energy placed in my life for a season to bless me in many special ways? I don't know the answer to that question now, but one day I will. One thing I do know for certain. Every life is precious, and they can touch us in special ways, sometimes in ways that are life changing and sometimes in ways that let us know for certain that angels exist.

> If you make the Most High your dwelling—even the Lord, who is my refuge—then no harm will befall you, no disaster will come near your tent. For he will command his angels concerning you to guard you in all your ways. (Psalm 91:9–11)

REFLECTIONS

CHAPTER 22

When Is It Too Late?

I had just arrived back at our inpatient unit when one of the nurses asked me to see one of her assigned patients. The patient was a forty-year-old female who had been crying almost nonstop since early that morning. The patient had been brought into the inpatient unit for pain management and would be returning home once that had been accomplished. Her request to her family was that she be allowed to die at home. She was in the final stages of her battle with cancer, and she would probably not be with her family much longer. She had two young children, and I thought to myself that leaving them must have been heavy on her heart.

When I arrived at her room, I found that she was alone. Her family had stepped out for some lunch. As the nurse had reported, the patient, Mandy, was crying softly. Her eyes were red and puffy, her hair unkempt, and her face was very pale. I introduced myself as the chaplain and asked if it would be okay if I sat with her a while. She seemed pleased that she had someone to talk with and would not be alone in the absence of her family.

I pulled a chair close to her bed so she would not have to look up to see me, and I softly asked why she was crying. I didn't receive the answer I had expected. Mandy told me that she had been raised in the Catholic Church but had not been active for many years. She was raised to believe that no one could know for certain they would go to heaven when they died. Now that she was dying, she feared that because she had not been a "good Catholic" she would go to hell. She was afraid that it was too late for her to do anything about it.

While Mandy was also hurting for her husband and children, she knew that they would be all right without her. Her husband was strong, and he loved their children passionately, so she was confident that, while they would certainly grieve, in the end they would eventually be able to move forward with their lives. Mandy had accepted the fact that she was soon going to die, but the thought of this terrified her when she thought of all the horrors of hell she had heard about as a child. This was the overwhelming concern for her as her time neared, and she even felt guilty for that.

I assured Mandy that it was not too late for her. I asked if I could share what the Bible had to say about how to know for certain she would go to heaven when she died. She was very agreeable, and I could tell that she was hoping I would have a lifeline to throw to her as she was sinking into the sea of hopelessness. Very quietly, but very clearly, I began to share verses of scripture with her that explained that we were all sinners. Then I told her how we could have all our sins not only forgiven but forgotten by God. I explained that it was only through our faith in Jesus, the Son of God, and His atoning work on the cross, that we could receive eternal life and know for certain that heaven was our home. I ended by quoting Romans 10:13, which says, "Everyone who calls on the name of the Lord will be saved."

I asked Mandy if she had understood what I had said, and she indicated with a nod of her head that she had. I also asked if she had any questions, and the only one she had was "What do I need to do now?" I explained that she must ask the Lord to forgive her of her sins, to come into her life as Lord and Savior, and to give her the gift of eternal life. But I also explained that she must truly believe what we had discussed and sincerely mean the words she was saying. She said that she understood, so I held her hand and led her in a prayer of confession and repentance as she received Jesus into her life as her Lord and Savior.

When we finished, I asked Mandy once again if she had any questions. She responded that she had no questions. With a beautiful smile on her face, she said she felt as if the weight of the world had been lifted off her shoulders. She felt clean and free for the first time in her life. She was so thankful that she could have the peace of knowing she would go to heaven. Mandy was like a completely different person from the one I had encountered when I first entered the room. I told her how happy I was for her, reiterating that God is so good and so merciful. We chatted for a few more minutes as we waited for her family to return.

I was still sitting at her bedside and holding her hand when her husband walked through the door. He had a very puzzled look on his face as he saw a strange man holding his wife's hand, while she had a big smile on her face. When he left, she had been crying, and now she was all smiles. I quickly introduced myself to her husband and told him that I was just leaving because I thought his wife had something very important she wanted to share with him.

As I walked down the hall, I prayed that he would be happy with her and for her. I also prayed that Mandy, in the short time she had, could be a positive influence for Christ with her family.

Mandy died at home a couple of weeks later. I am thankful that I will see her again one day in heaven. I hope the same will be true for her family.

LIFE LESSON

People often asked me, as a hospice chaplain, if I saw many "deathbed confessions." Sadly I had to answer, "No." I was always amazed at the fact that most terminally ill patients were more concerned about what would happen to their loved ones once they were gone than they were about what would happen to themselves when they stepped into eternity.

More than once I was asked by family members if I could talk to their dying loved ones about heaven. They wanted to know for sure that heaven would be their eternal destination. Unfortunately, I could only do this if the patient asked or gave permission. Other family members wanted to know when it was too late for a loved one to "get things right with God." Only God knows the heart or how long He will call to an individual, but because He is such a loving and merciful God, I believe He will woo almost all people until they take their very last breath. If they are in a coma, I believe that His Spirit will call to that person's spirit until the very end. I believe this so strongly that on more than one occasion I have leaned over the bed of a patient in a coma and whispered into his or her ear, encouraging them to call on the name of Jesus while there was still time. Did any of them hear me and do as I had encouraged them to do? I can only hope so, but I won't know for sure until I arrive in heaven, where I hope to see every one of them.

> This is good, and pleases God our Savior, who wants all men to be saved and to come to a knowledge of the truth. (1 Timothy 2:3–4)

REFLECTIONS

Conclusion

Death is a mystery. Even though there have been many books written in recent years about near-death experiences and trips to heaven and back, death remains a mystery. Over the years, I have watched many people take their last breath, often with my hand resting on them as I prayed for them. I have heard the sigh of that last breath as their spirits left their bodies behind that had been ravaged by age and disease or injury. I have seen people struggle to the end, and I have seen many go so quietly and peacefully.

As I have related in this book, I have seen many things that affirm to me there is a life after death. When a person takes that final breath, the body ceases to function, but the spirit lives on in another realm. Of course my faith and my acceptance of the literal translation of scripture lead me to believe as I do. This includes the belief that there is a heaven and a hell and that a person's spirit will go to one or the other of these places based on whether or not they have placed their faith in Jesus Christ. I understand that everyone who reads this book will not believe the same as I do, but I still hope the actual events I have recorded will bring you some comfort and peace when you are faced with the final journey of a loved one, or even your own. I also hope they will encourage you to evaluate where you are spiritually and what your eternal destination will be. We all have an appointment with God—an appointment that cannot be avoided.

Each life journey we are witnesses to, or experience personally, provides lessons from which we all can learn. I encourage each of you to begin observing each life with that approach. You will be surprised at how doing so will change your perspective on life and on death. And who knows? You might even recognize an angel along the way, one you would have missed otherwise!

> For the perishable must clothe itself with the imperishable, and the mortal with immortality. When the perishable has been clothed with the imperishable, and the mortal with immortality, then the saying that is written will come true: "Death has been swallowed up in victory." "Where, O death, is your victory? Where, O death, is your sting?" The sting of death is sin, and the power of sin is the law. But thanks be to God! He gives us the victory through our Lord Jesus Christ. (1 Corinthians 15:53–57)

In closing, I feel compelled to challenge you with one other thought. I wrote earlier in this book about heroes. Who are your heroes? Are they the celebrities, the professional athletes, the power brokers in business and politics? If so, maybe it's time to reconsider your answer to this question. Think about all our first responders and those in the military service who would give their lives for you. Many already have. How many of those other people would do that?

I have another question for you, one that is really going to get personal. How about Jesus? Is He your hero? More importantly, is He your Lord and Savior? After all, He has already given His life for you. How does He compare to the first group of people I mentioned? Got you thinking? I hope so.

If any of these real-life stories have touched you in a special way, or if any of them have revealed to you a life lesson other than the ones I have noted, please give them careful consideration. Thank you and may God bless you and grant you peace on your own spiritual journey.

Printed in the United States
By Bookmasters